CANC
ALIVE AND KICKING

By Steve Parton

To My Good
Friends

Barb & Joe

Love,

Steve

Permission has been given by most of the friends, and all the professionals named in this book. All names are real, with the occasional exception, when someone was particularly stupid or crazy.

Edited by Andie Parton and Sheelagh Wood
Editorial readers: Rob Bell, Helen Bartley, Jessica Veter, Marissa Slaven

Cover photo by Andie Parton
Cover design by Jordyn Campbell

Please visit www.partonbooks.com

ISBN-13: 9781094867922

~ This book is dedicated to my Isabel, for
reasons that will be made known upon reading ~

PREFACE

Prior to publishing the first book about my cancer journey, I had to contact almost eighty people for permission to use their names. I gave them but two choices: I could use the name, or I could change it. In the latter scenario, I still had every intention of using the anecdote, only with a different name; I did not give the option for the passages to be removed entirely. For Book 2, I decided not to do any of that jazz. There are medical people named and, in each case, I'm simply talking about the wonderful things they did to save my life or make it easier to make my way through this illness. I'm just assuming they are okay with being mentioned in the book. My friends know they're in the book, and they're okay with it. Every now and then, someone says (usually with a beer in hand), "You're not putting this in your stupid book, are you?" I reply: "Of course not; this is about my cancer journey, not about your hijinks."

~ INTRO ~

December 22, 2018

I was first diagnosed with kidney cancer in 2013. Over the next couple of years, I wrote a book called *Cancer Trip: Curing Cancer with Humour, Pot and Chemo*. I finished it at the end of 2016, leaving things on a relatively high note, with good hope for the future. I had a book release party in my hometown of

Dundas, Ontario, Canada (along with some other writer friends of mine), and the event was a resounding success.

This book is my follow-up. In writing this sequel, I will talk about all the crazy things that have happened, and the people I interacted with over the past two years. As the title of my last book suggested, I had consumed a great amount of pot—cannabis oil, to be precise – and it appeared to be instrumental in making the tumours shrink and, in a few cases, disappear.

At one of my book promotion events, a young fellow purchased the first book of the night. As he handed me the money, he said, "And where do the proceeds from this book go?" He stared at his money, still in my hands. I almost said, "I take it to the casino..." Then I thought about explaining how, after modest book sales, my earned wage works out to about $1.25/hour. In the end, I went with, "I haven't decided yet."

He seemed content enough with that.

2016

WARNING: This first entry, although it's lots of fun, is rather graphic. Feel free to skip it, if there's a chance you'll get offended. The remainder of the book is not quite as bad, and I'm fully clothed for most of it.

December 7

Wednesday was one of the worst nights of my life. I spent most of the entire night on the floor of my bathroom. I hadn't had a bowel movement in five days, and at 10 PM that night, I found myself trying to move a football (or what seemed like a football-sized BM). My wife, Isabel, was at work on night shift (she's a nurse), so I woke up some friends to help, or at least share in my horror. My friends Cam and Sally came right over. After a bit of chuckling over my predicament, I sent Cam to one of the overnight drug stores nearby. I asked him to pick up a package for Steve Parton from the pharmacist at the back of the shop. Next, I called the pharmacist to discuss the brand and type of enema I was to use. She put the little box in a small bag, and onto the counter, where it awaited pick-up. Shortly, Cam arrived at the drug store and asked for the package under my name. He then turned to leave, heading to the cashier. This was when he heard the pharmacist's voice behind him: "Not so fast."

She reached over, took the bag back and said, "There are a couple of things to know when using this product." To Cam's horror, she recited the 'things to know when using this product.'

"Make sure this is inserted firmly into your friend's anus." She gently shook the bag. "It's best if your friend is naked, and on his hands and knees when you do this."

Oh no. Cam's smile wiped itself from his face as he made his way back to his car. And on his way back to our neighbourhood he said to his dashboard, "Steve's a buddy and all, but I don't think I can do this."

When Cam arrived, to his relief, he learned that Dr. Brian was at my house. I had called my friend Brian when Cam was out on his mission. I could see the relief wash over Cam's face when he learned that Dr. Brian wasn't a psychiatrist or a paediatrician, but was in fact an Emergency Room doctor. Cam passed over the bag as if it had a small turd in it. "I think this is for you," he said.

The rest of the story is too graphic even for this book.

December 13

I've been lucky to have such wonderful doctors and nurses. Even my pharmacy is awesome. There is a particular young fellow who works at my local Shoppers Drug Mart, name of Stephen. He rocks, and he's very smart. When I call the pharmacy, I usually hope for him to answer. The conversation sometimes goes like this:

"Hey. It's me. I need a refill of one of my drugs. I don't know what it's called, but I can tell you how it makes me feel, and maybe you can figure it out from there."

"No problem, Steve. Bring it on."

2017

January 2

To me, there are many factors to consider when trying to rid the body of cancer. First, it's about having faith in your doctor. There are small things I do to help everything along. I continually try to will the cancer away. I also talk to my pills before consuming them. Don't worry, it's not a two-way conversation; they don't talk back. But before I take my chemo and cannabis oil pills, I remind them of the job they have to do. Also, I've researched many alternative treatments over the years. It's important to acknowledge that all modern mainstream medicine was considered to be alternative at one time in the past.

January 3

I've been taking night-time cannabis for a long time, and sometimes it keeps me up at night. At times, I wake Isabel up in the middle of the night, like when I'm ill, or when I've seen something hilarious while surfing the Internet in the early hours of the morning. At 3 AM, I found a humorous poster for a fictitious *Star Wars* movie. It wasn't actually that funny, but to my altered mind, it was a scream.

Isabel didn't wake up from my laughter; rather, it was from me shaking her shoulders. "Hmm?" she mumbled. "What is it? What's wrong?"

"Izzy, check it out. This is awesome." I showed her the movie poster on my phone. It had a picture of a silly little box droid. The text read, "It's a walking battery that repeatedly says 'Gonk`. But we made a movie out of it, and you will pay to see it. Because it's *Star Wars*."

Isabel then asked me if she could go back to sleep. "Sure," I replied. "If I find anything else funny, I'll let you know." Poor Isabel.

January 5

For some crazy reason, I became depressed. It was an extremely foreign concept for me, as I've been able to find happiness pretty much every day of my life. Catharine Munn is the mom of one of my star guitar students, and she agreed to talk with me. Luckily for me, she is a well-respected psychiatrist. In our conversation, Catharine told me I was depressed. When I asked why she felt that, she pointed out that I'd cried twice already in front of her. She knew I was taking great amounts of cannabis, and she pointed to that as something that was exacerbating my depression. The solution was easy – I had to get off pot. I wasn't so sure about that, owing to the fact that cannabis seemed to be keeping me alive.

A few days later, I had an appointment with my oncologist, Dr. Anil Kapoor. He showed me my latest CAT scan, and I learned that the tumour (located near my aorta), had grown. Also, it had spread to my lungs. He told me the chemo that I'd been on for two years was no longer working, and that I needed to stop taking it. He also suggested I stop taking pot. (More on my next drug treatment plan to follow).

It was interesting that Catharine had said the same thing to me, only days before. When I mentioned to her that I was not addicted to weed, and that I could stop anytime, she replied, "No you can't. It's nice that you feel you're not emotionally addicted, but your body definitely is. You need to wean off of it slowly." And so I arranged a sliding dosage schedule, to be implemented over the next month. After four weeks, I proclaimed myself to be free of marijuana – and then I became very ill. I realized that I had weaned too quickly. In the end, it took six weeks.

January 7

Sometimes my humour is on the dark side, because of the cannabis. This becomes a problem at times. I own a music school called Avalon Music Academy. Recently, I had been emailing back and forth with a lady who was considering signing up her two kids for piano lessons with us. After the fourth email, asking questions about the scheduling of the lessons, I typed out this reply:

"Jeezus, mang. Why do you gots to bother me all the live-long day? Just pick a damn time. It's only piano lessons. Fuck."

Before I could hit Send, I giggled myself silly. Surely, this mom would find my email hilarious. Isabel, in the next room, shouted over, "What's so funny this time?" I read the email aloud, and then I hit Send. Isabel shouted, "NO! You can't send that!"

For many years, I've been using Gmail, which has a function that allows you to change your mind within five seconds of sending an email. At the behest of my wife yelling at me from the next room, I gathered together just enough brain cells to click on "UNDO".

Then I argued with her. "Are you sure? It's pretty funny."

"I promise you it's not." It's a good thing I know to listen to my wife. I rewrote the email, removing all the "funny" parts. Maybe the lady doesn't want to be called "Mang" after all.

January 9

When I was first diagnosed, I wanted nothing to do with anyone else who had cancer. I guess I didn't want anyone to bring me down, in the face of my efforts to remain positive. But recently, while in line at the blood clinic at the Juravinsky Cancer Centre in Hamilton, I saw a poster advertising a support group called "Men's Night In, for Men Over 40 with Cancer". I decided to go give it a shot, take a chance to hang out with other cancer patients. Plus, they had pizza. As it turned out, they are a fantastic bunch of guys. I'm the baby of the group. We do indeed discuss our respective woes with cancer, but we mostly talk about guy things. It's a great time. Tibor, one of the fellas, came up with the expression "Brothers in the Trenches" to describe us all. It's quite fitting.

February 7

People are very kind to me. Banana oatmeal muffins have been delivered to my doorstep this evening, with no note or anything. I don't know who to thank, or who to blame if they turn out to be poisonous. I'll have Isabel taste one first, just in case.

February 21

After two years of taking cannabis oil as far as I could, I am now off it. I believe (as does my doctor, with some pause), that the pot was instrumental in the tumours shrinking as much as they did. Now I'm sleeping better. And I just need to figure out a way to get the rest of the tumours gone. The next thing in line is immunotherapy, a new, cutting-edge cancer treatment. But the costs are not covered, and Trillium Ontario won't pay for it. So I have to figure something else out. In the meantime, my doctor is arguing with the legislature people to fund it, and he's after the pharmaceutical company to lower the damn price. He's also researching other new drugs that are affordable and effective. Until then, I need to refocus my energies. And so I've been spending time working out the details of my victory party, for when the cancer is gone.

February 24

Tomorrow night, there will be a book-launch event for a few authors, members of the Dundas Writers' Group. We are expecting a full house, at Dundas' Gerstein Centre for the Arts. To promote the event, I did an interview with my friend Jeff Mahoney, who writes for *The Hamilton Spectator*. Jeff wrote an amazing article, talking about my music, my writing – and a little bit about the cancer. Craig Campbell also wrote a nice article for *The Dundas Star*. I was a celebrity in my hometown, if only for a few minutes.

February 25

This day couldn't get any better. I've been receiving messages wishing me luck for the book release event tonight. And I just received an email from Geddy Lee, the bassist and vocalist of Rush, my favourite band. By way of a mutual friend, Geddy received *The Spectator* article in which I spoke of my love of Rush. And he emailed me, wishing me luck for tonight, and thanking me for supporting Rush all these years. It put me on an emotional high. (No, I can't share his email address...)

February 28

My new treatment is now going to be covered by the Ontario Ministry of Health. I'm so pumped at this good news. Things get rolling in about four weeks, and I'll be off this crazy chemo that I've been on for over two years. It has been very hard on me, physically, and it's made me very weak.

The new treatment is called immunotherapy. I'll be going to the Juravinski Cancer Centre every couple of weeks for an IV drip. Whereas the chemo was only meant to keep things at bay, this new treatment may actually cure the cancer. It's a one-in-five chance, but I'm good with that.

I had posted the above passage on Facebook, along with a photo of my smiling face, and an apology:

Sorry about the shirtless pic; the bruises on my arms are from Isabel. No, she doesn't beat me; they're from all the needles (blood thinners) that I take. Soon, I'll hopefully be able to gain some weight, and stop feeling like I got hit by a bus every day.

March 1

I read in the news about a young lady in Hamilton who was caught faking cancer. She shaved her head and her eyebrows, and then told everyone she had the disease. She managed to fool the Ontario government, and she received over $200,000 in disability payments. People rallied around her. They cooked her

13

meals, held benefit concerts to raise money for her, prayed for her, and gave her bucket-loads of love and attention. The woman is currently in prison, serving a two-year sentence.

There are other cancer fakers from this area. One girl defrauded all her friends into donating money for treatments that never took place. There are other cases of this happening elsewhere. In the US, a woman claimed she had cancer, but it wasn't to raise money – she simply wanted the attention.

These people drive me crazy. Since my diagnosis in 2013, I have received tons of support and love from friends, family and the wonderful Facebook community. And I would be mortified if even one person thought that I was making up this disease.

April 4

One thing about having cancer is that you end up with many other cancer patients in your life. There are those who become acquaintances, friends, people I need, people I love, all of whom have cancer. And we look out for each other, sometimes by giving direct assistance or love, other times by simply being aware of each other. When someone beats the disease, he or she is still in the "club", but it's like the person has moved on to the upper echelons; we can all celebrate in the joy. And when someone drops out of sight, doesn't show up to a support group meeting, or stops posting on Facebook, the rest of us start to worry. This month was particularly rough, as I lost four friends to cancer. It sometimes just makes me feel like I'm circling the drain, myself.

April 6

How quickly things turn around: I am now off chemo! My immunotherapy started today. And they've just raised the chances from a 20% success rate to 33%. The other main difference between the two treatments is in the side-effects. The chemo had three pages' worth—and the bottom half of the last page was the scary stuff: death due to heart failure, death due to kidney failure, death due to lung failure—and on and on. But the immunotherapy has only one half-page of side-effects: and they seem to be manageable (no more feeling like I've been hit by a truck every day).

May 5

My friend Donna Mykytyshyn-Nunan called me the other day. She asked me if I was interested in having a living wake. After a brief chat, I learned that it's just like a regular wake, only it takes place while the guest of honour is still alive. I figure an event like that is arranged only after the person knows he or she is at the end of their rope, that there is a finite timeline for the person's days. I replied that it could perhaps be a good idea. Donna was then happy to be in charge of the festivities. "Great!" she said. "Let's meet on Monday to plan it out!" I gave it more thought, but I had to put the brakes on things. I was, in fact, not at the end of my days, and I was planning not to have a use for a living wake for a long time, if ever. But I said she could help me plan my victory party when the time comes. Donna is amazing that way.

Then I got to really thinking about the premise of a living wake, and I decided I would not want to have one. It would be a large party, perhaps with lots of people there. I would be able to greet friends in the group but spend perhaps only 20 to 30 seconds with each person. That doesn't sound like a fun time. So, instead, I've been inviting people to come visit me, one at a time. A couple times a week, my front porch is occupied by a friend and me. It is acknowledged that there is the possibility that we will not see each other again. I've been digging through the archives, looking up people I haven't seen since college, high school, or even grade school. I've invited people I've worked with, made music with, or kissed. Poor Isabel has had to be introduced to more than one of my ex-girlfriends from days gone by.

Anyone who receives an invitation for a porch talk has to meet two criteria: I have to like the person a great deal, and it has to be someone who does not steal my energy. In the past, I've usually been fine with energy-suckers, as I'd always had energy to spare. But not these days. I absolutely cannot spend time with someone who takes away my energy. By this, I refer to someone who grabs on to me and starts a conversation with, "Oh my god, I am so upset that you are sick, you don't deserve this, I can't believe this is happening to you, I can't take it anymore, I pray for you every day, please tell me what I can do, etc." And then come the tears, at which point I need to find a way to console the person, explaining that he/she will be alright, and will make it through this. Other times, it's simply someone who comes over and dumps a heap of baggage and problems onto my lap. I become incredibly stressed just hearing about the person's issues with work, kids or relationships.

May 18

I recently learned that I have a new tumour. This one is in my spine. It is destroying my vertebrae and is painful enough that I have to go on opioids to help me deal with it.

Today, I had radiation on my back, to attack the tumour. Funny enough, the pain wasn't too bad last week but, since the radiation, my spine has been giving me a great deal of grief.

This evening I fell asleep on the couch. My 11-year old daughter Meghan (Maggie) logged into my Facebook account, posted a selfie, and wrote a little message:

Hello Facebook. First this is not Steve Parton, this is his daughter Meghan. He is sleeping right now. Thank you a million times for every nice word that you said.
You are right, cancer is one of the worst ways to die. My stepmom,Isabel and I love our papa more then anyhing we

17

are very upset that he might be dieing but we have to keep our sprits up. If my dad survives then we we will have a huge party at my dad's favourite restaurant, Collin's hotel and all of you are welcome to come and celebrate that this stupid canser is FINALLY gone.

When I woke up, I sent the kids to bed, and my computer started pinging with comments to Meghan's post. So I wrote the following reply:

Thank you, everyone, for the heartfelt comments you left on my daughter's post this evening. She will read the rest of them in the morning. I had spent the day in the hospital, and I was beat. As I slept on the couch, Meghan "hacked" my phone (she has the pin), but I've decided not to press charges, as she's so darn cute. She and I talk all the time, but it was fascinating for me to see exactly where her thoughts were at. Back when the cancer returned in 2014, my son said to me, "Dad, if you die, do I get your Les Paul guitar?" I am a very lucky man. Look, I keep up a brave face a great deal of the time, but sometimes it gets very difficult to stare down my lot. So I turn to Facebook—and you always come through for me. Every comment I read reminds me that I'm not alone in this. It's very rare, but sometimes I think about my funeral—there will be live music, and jokes to be shared. Other times, I plan out my "Kicked Cancer's Ass" party— there will also be live music, and jokes to be shared. I much prefer the latter scenario, so that's where I focus my energy.

May 21

Whenever I come upon a new symptom or side-effect, or when I engage in a new adventure with this disease, Isabel looks it up online, so we can be prepared for what's to follow. This isn't always a good thing. For starters, there's the inconsistent information that's gleaned from Dr. Google. We often have to wait for our next appointment with the oncologist who, to his credit, has (so far) refrained from replying with, "Good God, where the hell did you learn that?" The second problem with looking up maladies online is that we almost always come across the worst-case scenarios, regardless of the slim likelihood that I may experience them. After learning that the new tumour was in my lower spine (Lumbar 1, for those who understand/care about that sort of thing), and because I was experiencing frequent, horrible pain, Isabel apprised herself of some of the worst possible outcomes that could arise. And they are bloody bad. It's possible that a tumour in L1 could collapse the spine, resulting in the patient losing all control of the legs, and become wheelchair-bound for life. After I recovered from the horror of this consideration, Isabel went on to read that the patient would also be incontinent. That one needed a quick clarification, just to be certain.

"That's where you don't have a lot of notice to get to a toilet?"

"Not exactly," she explained. "It's where you have no control over your bladder or your bowels. You'd be wearing a diaper for life."

Then a horrifying thought struck home: what about our currently-awesome sex life?

"Nope. Gone." Isabel looked just as worried as I felt.

It's for this reason that doctors don't give out their home phone numbers to their patients. Otherwise, my doctor would surely have received a call from me right then and there: "Hi, it's Steve Parton. Sorry to wake you. Yes, I know it's 1 AM. Listen, am I going to be wearing a diaper for the rest of my life, and wondering if my wife is 'getting some' from Sean Bean? He's the actor from Game of Thrones and Lord of the Rings. He's Isabel's free pass. Also, will I be in a wheelchair for the rest of my life?"

In reality, I had to wait for my next appointment. There's always my mother, though. Although she's a retired medical lab technologist, she happens to know loads about all things medical. Plus, she often predicts the future—go ahead and doubt me on this one if you like, but this book isn't about her psychic skills. So I called my mother first thing in the morning, happy that she is an early riser.

"Mum, is my spine going to collapse? Will I be in a wheelchair for life and wear a diaper like the crazy slot players at the casinos do?"

"Gee, dear, what makes you think I know that? Have you been on Dr. Google again?"

"Yeah. I need your medical opinion and, more specifically, I need you to look into your crystal ball and see that I'm still walking, still peeing while standing over a toilet."

"Dear, you know it doesn't work like that. Besides, I don't have a crystal ball. I think you know that as well. But I wouldn't worry about it. I'm sure you'll be fine. The tumour is small, and they got it early."

I felt a bit more at ease, but I still thought that next Tuesday's appointment with the doc couldn't come soon enough.

May 22

I'd been taking opioids to combat back pain for a while, and I was a bit concerned about becoming addicted. I don't believe I have an addictive personality, but I understand that many people have become so dependent on opioids that it ruins their lives. I'd had a question about my dosages, and I called my pharmacy. They were busy, so I researched the information myself, on the Internet. When I typed in the word "Hydromorphone", the first suggestion that came up was, "Hydromorphone Street Price". That wasn't exactly what I wanted to find, but I figured that, if the drug doesn't work for me, we could at least get our money back by selling it on a street corner in downtown Hamilton. That could be kind of dangerous, so maybe I'll just get Isabel to do it for me.

I saw on the evening news that two men with guns robbed a nearby Shoppers Drug Mart (not the one that I always go to). The thieves demanded all the stores of Hydromorphone, the exact drug that I use. The newscaster explained that the drug is very addictive (I'd already figured that part out). I decided then that, although I like to share my adventures with the people on Facebook, I shouldn't mention the drugs I have in my house. If thieves can rob a pharmacy at gun point, I'm sure they'd have no problem trying to relieve me of my stash of opioids. <NOTE TO WOULD-BE THIEVES: As of this printing, I am no longer on opioids, so it would be a waste of time trying to rob me.>

May 23

My weight loss has gotten out of control. I lost a total of 80 pounds. Prior to cancer, I had been able to access my inner tough-guy, when the need arose. It was good to know that I could protect my family from any ne'er-do-well we may come across. And being a musician who frequently performs in bars full of drunk people, I was often able to diffuse a situation with my sober wit – and my 220-pound frame.

At my worst, I shrank down to 140 pounds. As of this writing, I am at 160, which gives me the body of Shaggy, from Scooby-Doo. "Like, zoinks, Scoob: I sure could use a Scooby-snack."

I'm not sensitive about my weight. I sometimes even share The Steve Parton's Weight Loss Program:

Step 1: get cancer

Step 2: stop eating altogether

Step 3: watch the pounds fade away

Funny enough, an article appeared in *Cosmopolitan* magazine describing a guaranteed method of losing weight. The writer explained that there's no dieting or exercise involved. And they showed a picture of a woman who looked pretty darn confident—and skinny. But in the body of the article, it was explained that the woman in question was diagnosed with cancer, and then was on chemo. That was her weight-loss program. Predictably, people were outraged. Me, I decided then and there to cancel my Cosmo subscription.

May 24

The pain in my spine was still excruciating. To make matters worse, I started getting incredible back spasms. As such, I was bed-bound. Isabel and I remembered that she was going to have to work night shift the following night (she is a nurse). That meant I would be alone for the evening, overnight, and again the next day, as she slept. I'd already been asking so much of my family, that I decided it was time to turn to Facebook for some help. Here is what I posted:

> *I'm trying to find someone to possibly do a sleepover at my house in Dundas. <Allow me to clarify, as there are so many ways this could be misconstrued.> I've been having some complications with the radiation, such that I am immobile. I haven't been out of bed since yesterday. Isabel has been waiting on me hand and foot, and has*

everything all set up in the bedroom for me. She is working nights tomorrow (Wednesday), and I can't be left alone. There is a chance that this issue could fix itself before then, but I'm wondering if someone actually wants to sleep in our spare bedroom, just in case. Duties would be limited to filling up the bedside water bottle, fetching meds, etc (nothing uncomfortable). It would be best if you are someone who has been here before, and possesses enough testosterone to endure a potential Star Wars marathon. No need to share this post, as it may not work out with friends-of-friends. (Anyone regretting following me on Facebook now...?)

Funny, I thought that by using the words "testosterone", "star" and "wars", I'd have made it clear that I preferred a male to do this job. My reasons were three-fold: I needed someone strong enough to be able to bear my weight, to help me get to the washroom. Second, each time I cry out in pain, I would prefer to do so in front of a guy than a lady. Lastly, even though my relationship with my wife is absolutely rock solid, it's about the optics. I didn't want to put her in a position where she has to wonder what's going on while I'm at home with a lady she doesn't know, while she's at work for the night. When I mentioned that last item to Isabel, she of course brushed it off. "Dear," she said. "You're not nearly as sexy as you think you are. Between the commode, the pee bottle, the cane, your inability to stand up or even sit up without grunting, I'd be comfortable if you were being looked after by Angelina Jolie for the night."

Nevertheless, a number of kind women offered their help. Some of them I knew in real life, others I did not. One young lady I don't know outside of Facebook offered to come over and run me a bath. But she wanted to join me in it. As it turns out, our tub just isn't big enough for two. And also, I am married.

Of the men who offered help, there were a few buddies of mine with whom I'd be comfortable, in my vulnerable state. There was also a guy who offered his help in the hopes of seeing me naked (yes, he actually said that). I think he only pretended to like *Star Wars*.

With all that settled, I realized I still needed someone for today. Isabel had a doctor's appointment, after which she had to have her two-hour pre-night-shift nap. So back to Facebook I went, trolling for someone to come over for the afternoon. I hated begging for help like that, but the plentiful replies let me know that people were happy to help, or were sorry to be unavailable.

Jay Burr offered to come over for the afternoon. I accepted, as he is a heck of a nice guy. He plays tuba and trombone, and is one of the hosts of the Dundas Music Club, along with Danny Medakovic. About two minutes before Jay was to arrive, I had a peculiar thought. I didn't really know him. We'd jammed together; he was a great musician and sound man. But I didn't *know* him. Being alone with whomever was at my house, I would be totally vulnerable, and completely subject to the person's honesty. He could empty my wallet in front of me, and there wouldn't be a thing I could do about it. He could load my guitars into his car, and I'd be helpless to stop him. So I telephoned Danny, Jay's and my mutual friend, to ask if Jay is an honourable man. As the line connected, Jay arrived at my front door, and let himself in, per my request. I couldn't very-well talk about Jay in front of him, so I ended the call, and decided to trust my earlier instinct. As it turned out, I made a new friend that afternoon: Jay was fantastic. He had no problems with my pee bottle, or any of my other silly requests. In front of him, I realized what might happen if I had the need to move my bowels. So I sent him down to my basement to fetch the commode. Neither of us discussed the possibility of my having to use it that day.

Shortly after Jay arrived, a nurse from the VON (Victorian Order of Nurses) showed up for my monthly check-up. Here's the thing: the opioids had swung into full gear, and I was high as a kite. The nurse was named Amandeep. She was great—kind and skilled. I tried very hard to be nice to her, but my drug-brain took over, and I found myself trying to be clever. I laughed, then cried, then called her "Sweetie-pie". I think the poor nurse took a bit of mistreatment from me, but she took it in stride. I'm pretty sure her notes in my chart were about warning the next nurse about me.

Over the next several months, she came over to look after me many times. She had actually asked me to just call her Aman, but I liked the long version of her name better. When I asked her if her parents and I were the only ones who call her Amandeep, she said "Nope. Just you."

Later that afternoon, when Jay got up to leave, I told him my earlier thoughts about my being subject to the honesty of my afternoon helper, and how we hadn't really known each other well, before this. He laughed, remarked that all that had changed, and offered to come back anytime, as we are now friends. In the end, I never used the commode. I don't know who was more relieved about that.

That evening, shortly before Isabel left for the night, Alan Hinckley showed up. Of all the people who offered to spend the night, I knew Alan would be great. He's the bass player for my band. He's a bit older than I am, he's seen and done everything, and nothing fazes him. He didn't even glance at the commode, sitting like a throne in the middle of the living room.

By bedtime, I was feeling a bit better, so I tried to see if I could get up the stairs for the night. With a great deal of help from Alan, I made it. He helped me get into bed, then sat and talked to me for a while. It's amazing how deep conversations about music theory can get. He then went to our spare room to sleep. A couple of times he rushed into my room when I called out for pain meds in the middle of the night. I apologized to him, as my late night howling may have sounded like I was having sex in there. He wasn't worried. "If that's what you sound like when you're having sex, one of us is doing it wrong," he replied.

In the morning, Isabel came home, and went up to the master bedroom. Alan was sitting beside me on the blankets, leaning against the headboard. We were discussing the importance of proper microphone placement in the recording studio. Isabel didn't bat an eye. "I think you're in my spot," she said to Alan. He left soon after, and Isabel slept off her long night shift.

James Gould and his brother Christian are two fine young men: smart, handsome and talented musicians. They attended my music school at an early age and studied with us for years. Now, they put out albums and make rock videos. James saw my Facebook post about needing some help, and he said he'd be available on Thursday, while Isabel slept off her shift. As with Jay and Alan, I had to give him the "detailed version" of what the job entailed. He confirmed that he was up for it, as he'd had a good deal of experience working with disabled children.

James arrived at 9am, in time to relieve Alan. Thankfully, I didn't have to use the commode. Unfortunately, this meant that I was still plugged up. There was not a lot for James to do. I moved beyond peeing in the bottle, as I could make it to the main floor washroom, provided James hauled me off the couch and took my weight during the journey. The poor guy found himself in the bathroom with me, hoping I didn't need him to drop my drawers and lower me down to the toilet. Another bullet was dodged, as I told him I could manage.

Back on my couch, I had several back pain attacks as I tried to adjust my position. Each time this happened, I yelled out. I'd explained to James that there's nothing that can be done, and that he didn't need to rush over. But one particular attack got out of control; it didn't subside after the usual 15-20 seconds, and I was really suffering. James saw it. This kind young man sat down on the couch beside me and held my hand until the pain went away.

May 30

It was a rough night. I finally had my back spasms under control, such that they didn't wake me up every time I moved. Around 2 AM, our crazy alpha male cat Marcus mistook my big toe for a mouse, a mouse that he had to destroy. His claws in my foot inspired my back to flare up, and I screamed out loud. I scared the bejesus out of Isabel. Then at about 5am, I got the hiccups. I had never really thought about this as being a problem; I hadn't anticipated it. But, with my wrecked spine, each hiccup felt like someone was whacking me in the back with a baseball bat. What a way for poor Isabel to wake up. Come to think of it, it's an awful way for poor Steve to be woken up, too.

I did manage to get a bit of sleep, but the hiccups returned. A Google search offered no help, so I turned to Facebook for ideas:

Does anyone have a reliable cure for hiccups? Before you reply with "Poor baby has the hiccups; life must be so rough!" please know that each hiccup feels like a baseball bat to the back—because I don't do anything small, of late! One of my new meds (for the radiation on my spine) has given this to me. I'm also hoping that no one says, "LMGTFY (Let Me Google That For You)", as I tried that. Peanut butter doesn't work, neither does holding my breath. A spoonful of sugar actually does work, but I can't be eating that all day long. I've also heard you can scare the hiccups away. So if you plan to hide in my closet and jump out, let Isabel know in advance, so you don't scare her too.

The hiccups lasted for days. I eventually learned they were caused by a medication I was taking, so my doctor arranged for an alternative.

June 3

As the owner of a music school, I spend a good deal of my time greeting people (students, their parents, my teachers), and making sure everyone gets to where they need to be. Sometimes a dad I haven't seen in a while will pop by the office to say hi and shoot the breeze. And it saddens me that I can't stand up, as standing on one's feet is a necessary element to shaking another man's hand. My father wouldn't have been happy about it either, were he in the same boat as I am. So my solution is to forego

31

handshakes, and hug people instead. I have since explained that handshakes are for strangers, as I pull someone in for a hug. Sometimes the person gets thrown off guard, especially as I am often seated on my walker at the time.

There are tasks I just cannot do on my own. Tying my boots is one such task. When I leave the house to go look after my school, my bootlaces often drag behind me, and I have to just hope that I don't trip on them. Knowing I can't go all day with my laces dragging about, I'll ask one of my teachers to step into my office and tie my boots. It's rather emasculating, but my friend Craig, one of the guitar teachers, was always happy to oblige, without question.

June 4

I read an article about how complaining is bad for us, bad for our souls. I have a bit of difficulty with this. It's not that I disagree; in fact, I subscribe very strongly to this premise, and I think the world would be a better place if more people adopted this attitude. But, of late, I've been instructed to make note of all the aspects of my ailments. I do this so the doctors can find a way to help me not die—and to help future patients with the same ailments. It's a license to complain—and I hate it. My wife has to listen to me list off the side-effect *du jour*, although she continually asks me to share. Sometimes I get so tired of this sort of complaining that I just stop mentioning what's going on. And then things creep up on me and become worse, and I get scolded for not addressing them earlier. As soon as I am cured, I resolve to revert back to my non-complaining lifestyle. I can't wait. Nor can my wife, I'm sure. In a discussion with my friend, the Reverend Duane Henry, he assured me that my type of complaining didn't fall into the specific category of being the "bad for your soul" type. He's a smart man, and a good friend.

June 4

Isabel came back from the drug store with new meds. The VON nurse was with me at the house.

I saw the "pill" she had with her.

"That thing's huge," I said. "How am I supposed to swallow that?"

"It doesn't go in your mouth," the nurse replied.

"Where does it—oh, no."

The nurse offered to insert it. I said I wanted Isabel to do it, maybe after the nurse left. She offered a second time. Look, although any man would be delighted at the idea of being naked around two ladies, getting something shoved up my butt kind of takes the excitement away. The next day I spoke with Deb, the pain management nurse. She asked about my BMs. I mentioned the suppository, and told her it wasn't nearly as fun as it sounds.

"Um, does it sound fun...?" she asked.

"Why do you hate me so much?"

For those not in the know, opioids make going for a BM a very difficult task.

June 5

I met a fellow named Joe Cleary on Facebook. We have the same type of cancer, and the same oncologist (Dr. Kapoor). Joe is a drywaller who has kids and grandkids. He is a nice man, and is very soft-spoken. Dr. Kapoor was holding a seminar for a group of about 25 pharmaceutical researchers, and he asked Joe and me to attend, to discuss our respective cancers and answer questions. We were both happy to oblige, though Joe was a tad nervous about the event.

Dr. Kapoor's assistant met Joe and me in the lobby of the hospital and accompanied us to a small amphitheatre. Kapoor, ever the gentleman, embraced us both. The three of us were seated on the stage area at the front of the room.

I whispered to Joe, "Why don't you go first? I have a habit of talking until peoples' ears fall off."

But Joe would have none of that. So I addressed the audience, and started discussing my cancer journey, from diagnosis until that morning, leaving out no details. I told lots of stories and jokes, and the researchers seemed genuinely interested in what I had to say. After about an hour and a half, I finished up.

It was then Joe's turn to speak. Poor guy. It turned out I was a tough act to follow.

June 6

I had my men's cancer support group tonight, but I was a bit late. This made some of the guys nervous, because if a member doesn't show up, it's entirely possible that he's dead, having succumbed to his cancer—or else he's just busy doing something else that night. I arrived seven minutes late, and all the guys cheered. It was peculiar, being cheered because I'm not dead.

June 11

I was very stoned on the opioids. For some reason, I figured that this was to be my last day on Earth. As Isabel helped me into bed, I told her matter-of-factly that I was dying.

Came the loving reply: "No, you're not. Let's get you into your bedclothes."

But all evening, I insisted that this was it for me. I was surprisingly calm about the prospect. Isabel wasn't so sure, and she actually smiled at me for a while. "Time to go to sleep; I'll see you in the morning."

"I hope so."

It turned out that she was right.

June 12

Sometimes I have to find joy in the little things. In my cancer support group, the guys were discussing the worst parts about having cancer. I said that it's my lack of a brown three-day beard, à la Indiana Jones (the chemo had turned my beard to white). The other guys had boring things, like fear of death, a daily run of the shits, etc. But I want my three-day beard back (not dying before my kids grow up was also one of my concerns). In any case, I'm rocking the five-o'clock shadow today, and so life is grand.

June 18

After church, most people congregate down in the dining hall for coffee time. This morning, after having juice and snacks, I headed out to the parking lot. But someone had parked a car behind mine, and I couldn't leave. So I returned to the church, and climbed up on to a chair to get everybody's attention. I shouted, asking who owned the offending car, but nobody answered. I then had another problem in that I was unable to get myself down from the chair. Right away, one of the ladies saw my predicament, and came over to help me down. I think it was Mrs. Wood. I had actually wanted Chuck, one of the men, to help me. Chuck's a manly man with a handlebar moustache. He could probably lift his pickup truck up over his head. But Mrs. Wood got to me first. "I'll help you down, sweetie. Be careful, now." I was so embarrassed.

June 19

I've learned the difference between being weak and being tired. I spend most of my days on the couch, not out of tiredness, but out of weakness. A kind neighbour came by to see how I was. Seeing me lying on the couch, she offered some advice: "You know what you need? You need to go out jogging. That'll do you some good." I was too tired to reply, so I told her I'd give it a try some time. I later came across an analogy to explain my weakness: sometimes, when I'm home alone (a rare occurrence, but nonetheless), I find myself on the couch, and I become thirsty. At our place, the kitchen is right next to the living room. Twelve steps will put me in front of the sink, in reach of nice, refreshing water. But I'm too weak to stand, let alone make it to the sink. And so, I just go without, at least until Isabel comes home. As for jogging, that's pretty-much out of the question.

June 20

Whenever I leave my house, I always carry a little emergency kit with some meds (painkillers, anti-nausea, etc.). This afternoon I went to work at my music school, and after an hour, I had a huge bout of pain. I reached into my kit and found that I was out of opioids. I would have called Isabel to bring me one, but she was asleep, being on night shift. I'd even considered giving my car keys to one of my teachers, so he could go to my house and pick up a pill for me. The problem there was that my meds were kept by the side of my bed, and it wouldn't be very nice for Isabel to be awakened by a strange man in her bedroom.

And so I called up the local Shoppers Drug Mart. I was trying to send thought waves through the phone, so that my guy Stephen would answer. He is an incredible young man, as evidenced by the following story:

The phone picked up. "Hello, Stephen speaking." Instead of introducing myself, all I could say was, "Oh, thank God." Immediately, the reply I heard was, "Oh, hi Steve."

I told Stephen about my predicament. All I needed was one damn pill. I knew I was asking a lot, that this was a serious drug. But he made it happen. He saw there was a refill in the prescription for 60 pills. So he changed it to 59 pills owing, and had one for me, ready to go.

One of my teachers drove me to the pharmacy, but I knew she wouldn't be permitted to receive my pill. So I telephoned inside the store and asked for Stephen. He immediately came out, holding my pill and a cup of water. He stood there while I took the drug.

The next day, I felt much better. I returned to the drug store, but only because I needed to mail a letter. As I passed by the pharmacy counter, I then realized that I hadn't thanked Stephen for his help the previous night. I looked up, and there he was. I reached out my hand, and he gave me a fist-bump. All was good.

June 21

Through each stage of my cancer journey, I have been posting developments on Facebook. All posts, good or bad, are accompanied by a photo of me smiling. Sometimes it's a smile of a small victory, other times it's a smile of hope. Today, I had a little something to gripe about, as my meds were giving me grief.

So I composed a short paragraph, devoid of whining or complaining. The accompanying photo showed how I was feeling, with a grimace, rather than a smile. Among the encouraging posts, à la "Hang in there, Steve!" etc., there were two people who told me I needed to smile. Both of them went on to explain the importance of a positive attitude, and how it begins with a smile. One person was a stranger; the other was a friend from years back. In both cases, I was kind of pissed off. Since diagnosis, I've been walking around with an ear-to-ear smile, throughout the pain and misery, trying my damndest to see the good in all of this. And I have always tried to spread that happiness around. But I posted one damn photo without a smile, and (two) people got preachy. Sheesh.

June 22

One of the symptoms of the spinal tumour resulted in my wife's and my sex life coming to a screeching halt. After about Month Two, I offered to sub out my husbandly duties to someone else (but only on the condition that actor Sean Bean was available). Isabel found this rather funny, almost as if she were entertaining the idea. If the shoe were on the other foot, I would have to try and resist the urge to see if Christina Hendricks (the pretty secretary from Mad Men) is up for helping me out. Time to exercise patience. This isn't going to last forever. Shit, I sure hope it doesn't last forever.

June 23

This afternoon I was by myself. Actually, I wasn't totally alone. Isabel was sleeping off her night shift, so I'd be able to wake her up in case of an emergency, like if I forgot what channel Much Music is on, or if I couldn't find my favourite slippers.

On my couch, I was in so much pain that I couldn't move, and I had to pee. Often, when I need some help, I turn to Facebook, knowing that someone will offer up a ride, or help preparing food. For these things, it's okay to get on the Internet. Even though lots of people have invited me to call them directly if I need help, it's actually too much to contact each person individually. Plus, it puts people on the spot, making them feel badly if indeed they are unavailable. But this time, I knew I couldn't post, "Hi, everybody. I can't pee, so is there anyone who can accompany me to the toilet, maybe hold me up so I don't dribble all over the floor?" Instead, I called people who live nearby. My friend Kevin, who lives down the street from me, came right over to help. It's a helluva way to bond, when one man helps another man take a pee. Most guys would agree that it's actually better to bond over beer, billiards, or a hockey game.

June 24

I have a gig tonight at The Cat and Fiddle with my rock band, The Relics (I'm the guitarist/vocalist of the band). It's going to be a bit of a problem, because I was in so much damn pain this afternoon that I couldn't move. Isabel was sleeping off nights, so I called Kevin over again to come and help me up from the couch. He filled me up with my painkiller drugs—and now I'm frickin' stoned. This is going to be a crazy gig—and it's also the Avalon Music Academy staff party. Don't tell the guys in my band, or they'll probably replace me.

June 25

It was a Sunday, and I was at home, alone with my 11 year-old daughter, Meghan, and I was pretty-much paralyzed on the couch. Around suppertime, I told Meghan I'd guide her through cooking supper, as the kitchen is right next to the living room, where I knew I would remain for some time yet. I guided her through filling a pot with water, turning on the gas stove, and watching the water boil for our macaroni and cheese feast. It turned out that she hadn't filled the pot with enough water, and the noodles got burnt. So I called our neighbour Jodi to come over and help. She and her husband have three kids of their own, and I knew she'd be busy making supper for her family. But she came right over and saw the disaster that was our kitchen. Straight away, she took Maggie over to her house. They returned a short while later with supper for the two of us and a bag lunch for Meghan to take to school the next day. I have great neighbours.

June 27

Since the cancer spread to my spine, I've been having a great deal of trouble. My doctor said there was a risk of my spine collapsing, the result of which I would be paralyzed from the waist down. This would also mean I'd be incontinent (and would have to wear a diaper), and there'd be no more sex. So today I spent the day at the Juravinski Cancer Centre. They did an MRI, performed some magic, and the result was that my spine is not collapsing, I'll be able to have sex any old time I like, and I'll still be able to use a toilet. Life is grand.

Since I stopped the chemo and started with immunotherapy, I had to switch oncologists. Dr. Kapoor's friend and colleague is

Dr. Sebastien Hotte. Like Dr. Kapoor, Dr. Hotte is revered throughout the world's medical community for his work in cancer treatments.

June 30

It's been a helluva day: three days since I've slept, two days since I've eaten, three days since the last BM and, worst of all, SIX days since I've played my guitar! Yesterday morning was day three of my near constant "gunshot attacks" (spasms, seizures of my spine and legs). Isabel came downstairs to my couch. I'd been up nearly the whole night, doing a great deal of screaming. With Isabel by my side, I told her I'd given up, that I have no more strength, and I'm just too tired to fight off the attacks any more.

My spinal problems were getting worse, and I started to walk and feel like a crotchety old man, hunched over on a cane or walker. Then I started having back spasms every time I moved, adjusted my position, or if someone touched me. This meant that Isabel couldn't put her hand on me as she is wont to do. It didn't make for a good marriage, when she would forget, and touch my shoulder. I'd scream in pain, and yell "Don't touch me!" We'd finally had enough. I went to Emergency the next day. We saw a specialist who, after viewing my MRI, said I needed orthopaedic surgery.

Things were getting complicated. Even though I'd learned that I won't be paralyzed, I still had to wait for surgery to fix my spine from where the tumour was. It felt as if someone was standing behind me with a gun. Every half hour or so, he would shoot me in the back. It wasn't a big gun, maybe a .22—but I wasn't happy about it. I knew that Isabel would not actually let someone just walk in and shoot me, even if he asked politely.

I was able to keep the attacks at bay, but only if I concentrated. I could feel them starting to build up, so I just relaxed and willed them away. But I had to be awake to do this: if I drifted off to sleep, I got attacked, and I woke up screaming. As such, I'd slept only a couple of hours over the past three days. Each time I started to drift off to sleep, a dream began, almost instantly (as my body was aching to dream). Then, when my guard was let down, I got attacked. The drugs did not seem to be working anymore.

This night so far has been pretty bad. I was glad to learn that I am unlikely to become a paraplegic. But the tumour in my spine (and the subsequent radiation) is still giving me loads of grief. It's 3:00 AM now. I woke up an hour ago with huge mofo pain. I couldn't move, which was a problem, as I also had to pee. Isabel was at work, so I had no choice but to shout for my children, sleeping down the hall. Those poor kids. They shouldn't have to bear any aspect of my burden; they shouldn't have to nurse their father. Meghan woke up first, and came groggily into my room. I

44

had to send her downstairs to get my pain pills—and my pee bottle. I'm not even sure she knew what it was, other than the funny-shaped bottle on the living room side table (no wonder we don't get return visitors at our house). After Maggie delivered the bottle and pills and returned to her room, I rolled over onto my side—and screamed in pain again. She came racing back, suggesting we call an ambulance. I told her we didn't need to.

"But Dad, I've always wanted to call 911! Please, can I call them? They might even bring a fire truck!" She's a Parton, alright, able to see the exciting side of everything: Dad is ready to keel over, but she gets to wave to the firemen. In my stupor, I actually thought to myself, "Well, anything for my little girl..." As it was, I sent my daughter back to her bed. That was an hour ago. The pain meds started to kick in, so naturally, I decided to share my adventure on my Facebook page. My readers soon realized that sober people don't tell bladder stories.

July 1

I had spasms from my spine all day long. We had plans that I would go to the hospital this day. I did not want to go last night, as it's very hard to wait in Emergency overnight.

And I had another problem in that it was time to arrange for the teachers at my music school to get paid. So I asked my friend Helen to come over. She is from England, and was my assistant at my music school—I had to reach out to everyone regarding their paycheques. Normally, I look after this on my own, but I was pretty useless, prone on the living room couch and all. The first thing I needed from Helen was for her to be a secretary, to take a letter. It was a missive to all the teachers, giving options for picking up their cheques or receiving E-transfers. I started to dictate the text, but Helen interrupted me.

"Wait a minute! It's July 1st. We have to start by acknowledging Canada Day!" I lost my train of thought, but I agreed. Then I fell asleep, so Helen took the initiative, composing the letter on my behalf, writing in my stead.

After a few minutes, Helen woke me up to read me her masterpiece. At the first line, I knew I was in trouble. It started thus: "Have a lovely Canada Day, Everyone!!!!!" I had to explain that the word 'lovely' was not in my vocabulary, and that an exclamation mark has no place in a business letter. And a stream of five exclamation marks belongs in no letter. Helen was a little disappointed, so we came to a compromise – with two exclamation marks. Helen went on to explain that, if the teachers could reply regarding payroll, that would be tickety-boo. I was too tired to argue, so the letter, with my name attached, was sent out as Helen wrote it.

After Helen left, we decided it was time to go to the hospital, as the spasms were more than I could bear. We realized that I couldn't just be driven to the hospital, as there was no way I'd be able to get into a car. So we called an ambulance, and I loaded up on painkillers. When it arrived, and I saw the paramedics rolling my stretcher out to the front of my house, I noticed that their vehicle was blocking the entire street, in both directions, so no cars could get through. I decided then never to complain about the neighbours taking up too much parking on the road.

In my living room, I lay on my couch, frightened of what was going to happen. Isabel explained to the paramedics that I will fly into a horrible spasm if anyone touches me. But, of course, they would need to transfer me to their stretcher. I told them to do what they had to do, no matter how much I hollered. They were ever so professional and understanding of my situation. They slid me like a pizza from my couch to the stretcher, and I yelled like a banshee. After a few moments, it was over, and I calmed down.

Out in front of my house, the paramedics started to wheel me towards the back of the ambulance. I held up my hand and shouted, "Stop! We can't leave yet; I have to say goodbye to my neighbours. Can you bring me to each of their doors?" I heard a voice say, "You don't have to; we're here." I looked up to see the sweet smile of my friend Karen, who had walked here from down the street. Other doors opened, and Cam and Rich emerged from their houses to see me off.

Being in the Emergency Department of the hospital was a problem, as I'd made plans for that afternoon to get together with three close friends from high school. William, Mike and Corey are some of the smartest, most noble men I know. Our yearly get-togethers are legendary.

Lying on a gurney in ER, I knew I had to cancel my plans with the boys. I also had to contact my family, let them know where I was at. So I composed an email on my phone to send out to all of them. When it comes to composing text, I am rather OCD about it. Every sentence must be without flaws. My friends and family knew my habits well, and so they knew that something was amiss when I sent out the following email:

Can yo all contact each other? For two visits: One visit from the family, and one visit from the Fred's they are all attached Is clear? Chis will arrange the family, well William will arange the boys.
Isabel will email the location. In at Juravinski Hospital ER,
Im no very good hostess.

Apparently, I had taken too many of the painkillers. I have a vague recollection of writing this on my phone, and of proofreading it before sending it out. Something in my drug-addled brain proclaimed that the message was just fine, and so I hit SEND with confidence. William, Mike and Corey read my email and knew something was wrong. They decided to come straight to the hospital.

I was in Emergency for almost 24 hours before I was admitted. I spent much of that time asleep. During the afternoon,

I awoke to find Tomas and Norma Chavez at my bedside. They are from El Salvador, and Tomas is the custodian at our church. With his thick Spanish accent, Tomas wished the grace of God on me. They were very kind, and they had a good cry with me when they saw my condition.

Alan, my bass player friend, showed up to see me at the ER as well. I told him not to touch me, as I didn't want another spasm. Then I came up with an idea: I gave Alan my phone, and asked him to shoot a video when the paramedics try to move or adjust me. I knew that I would then fly into a spasm, and I wanted video evidence of the fact, to show people who didn't believe me. The hospital staff was actually not happy seeing Alan videoing everything with my phone: "Sir, put that away," one of them said.

In the days leading up to my hospital stay, I had a moment of clarity during which I wrote a short note to give to anyone in case I was unable to access my un-crazy side. I kept this letter with me, and often showed it to the nurses:

Hi. This note was written by the not-stoned Steve. Please share with anyone currently witnessing, or being affected by, my meltdown:

I have been taking very powerful meds to combat issues related to cancer. The result is that sometimes the meds get me horrifically stoned. I'm not in control of my mind when this happens. I say and do things I don't mean, but I'm harmless as a kitten. Don't think for a moment that I enjoy being like this, because I do not.

Rest assured, I'll probably apologize to you tomorrow, though I won't remember much of what I did or said today. Please just get me home. Or call my wife, Isabel.

And please give me my phone back.

Yours,

Not-Stoned Steve

July 3

Things have been better since they admitted me to the hospital. The doctors conducted their sleuthery to try and figure out what was causing the spasms, and what they could do about it. They never found out exactly what had been happening to me, why the spasms were happening. Really, it came down to the administering of some high-test drugs (opioids). For instance, they gave me drugs for muscle spasms and one for nerve pain. I didn't care, as long as the crazy spasms stopped.

We waited in the hospital for a few days to see if the drugs would start to work. They did and, after a week, I went home. There were several things that happened in the hospital, which I will now relate.

My roommate was a man in his 60s named Bert. He was having a very hard time with things. I didn't ask him what his ailment was, but he was very grumpy to everyone who waited on him. He eventually picked up on the fact that the staff appeared to be giving me better treatment.

"Hey you," he started. "What the hell is wrong with me? The nurses seem to like you better." I explained that I showed gratitude for every person who entered our room. I went out of my way to try and make things pleasant for every nurse, medical student, orderly—including the people who bring me food or empty the garbage pail. It only takes a few moments to engage someone, ask about his/her day, etc. Before long, I knew everyone's names. In some cases, I learned about their spouses, boyfriends and girlfriends, their kids, their music preferences, and so on.

To his credit, Bert decided to try and take a page from my playbook. He was actually very funny. I heard him buzz the nursing station asking for some water.

"Please," I said to him.

"What?" he asked.

"You forgot to say please. Call her back." So he did. I continued, "When she gets here with your water, ask her how her day is going, or tell her she looks nice in her outfit."

Bert was confused. "But I don't care how her day is going. She has a job to do."

"Well, just try it, and see what happens."

The nurse arrived with Bert's water. He took it and said to her, "You look hot in them pants." Without replying or reacting, the nurse left his water and took her leave. Bert grinned at me. "When does the great treatment start?" he asked.

July 4

I was sitting up in the bed in my room in the hospital, and things were good. I was all drugged up, I felt better, and I was just waiting to figure out what was going to happen to me. Several very kind people had been asking Isabel and my family which hospital I was at. But I absolutely did not have the energy for visitors. Just saying hello for a few minutes would drain me. All that would happen is that the well-meaning visitor would see me scream off my attacks (my friend William can attest to the fact that they're horrifying), and it wouldn't be a fun time.

Later that afternoon, I was visited by a young resident to discuss my blood thinners, administered by needles. They'd had trouble securing my brand of choice, so the girl said they were going to replace it with a brand called Fragmin. The problem was that I'd had this brand before, and it seems to explode inside my skin. I tried to explain this to the resident, but she didn't seem to understand what I was talking about. So I told her that Fragmin was in fact made of molten lava.

"Really?" she asked.

"Yes. So please be a dear and find me some Innohep. It's my favourite kind of blood thinner." In the end, Isabel brought in some needles from our supply at home.

My roommate Bert has a cell phone with the loudest ringtone in the world. It's a song, with the opening guitar-build from Alice Cooper's "Under My Wheels": "Ba-na-na-na-na-na-na-na— Telephone is ringing..." It's crazy loud, and when it rings, Bert doesn't wake up – but I do. So I have to scream his name at him to wake him up. If I'm awake when it rings, it scares the crap out of me. If I'm asleep when it rings, it jolts me awake and sends me into a panic. But it's hard to complain, as I have had a line up of family visitors here, and Bert hasn't said a word about it. I've been having parties, and Bert doesn't say anything. Bert's own family came by one time, and they all gave him crap for his being there, and bitched about everything they could think of.

When his family left, Bert asked me again why the nurses seem to like me so much. I reminded him that I always say please and thank you. Also I learn their names.

Bert shook his head. "Oh, there's too many nurses here for that."

"No there aren't. We only have one at a time, and it's for twelve hours. And they write their names on the board on the wall. Today, we have Kelly. She's due here soon. Let's try it together: 'Thanks for coming in today, Kelly.'"

Bert wasn't convinced. "Thanks? But she ain't done nothing yet."

"Yes she did. She left her family to look after us, potentially wiping our butts. That alone deserves thanks."

So Bert learned to behave a bit better with the nurses. He saved his complaining for after the nurses left the room. In fact, he saved his complaining for me. And it came in a torrent. "The stupid nurses hate me. And she forgot to bring me another pillow like I asked. They're all just stupit."

I decided to change the subject. " Bert, can we talk about your cell phone ringtone? I love Alice Cooper, and—"

"Who's Alice Cooper?"

"He's the guy who sings the song on your phone, 'Under My Wheels.'"

"No, the song's called 'Telephone is Ringing.'"

Ah, Bert. It wasn't his fault that he didn't know better than to try and argue classic rock with me. But I let it go. The name of the song wasn't important.

"Well, anyway, could we make a deal? I love that song, whatever it's called, but the volume is loud enough to wake up a drunk tauntaun on a cold Hoth night."

"Kid, you speak some weird shit."

I smiled. "Yeah, well, could you turn the ringer volume down a bit? It's crazy loud."

"I don't know how."

"That's okay; I can do it for you."

"But you don't even know what phone I have."

" Bert, I'm a young guy, kind of. I can operate all cell phones."

"How about if I just keep it under my pillow?"

"I guess that'll do. I hope."

Bert wanted to shave, so the nurse gave him some shaving supplies, along with a single-blade Bic razor, the el-cheapo kind. I've used them before, and they're brutal. From Bert's complaining, I realized that he didn't like them either. He called out to me, "Man, they gave me better razors in jail!"

I got into a conversation with Louise, the nurse manager. She said there are currently ten people waiting for beds in this unit. I felt guilty about where I was. My bed was comfortable, the nurses were kind enough to laugh at my jokes, and I had everything I needed. I couldn't imagine sitting in a hard-back chair, waiting to be admitted to the unit. I told Louise to send me home, that I was all better, and I didn't need any more help. She smiled, and explained that if I went home too early, I'd be back soon, with worse problems. I was glad she said that, as I knew I was not ready to go home. I still had back spasms, though not as many, and I was in a great deal of pain. I decided to post an update on Facebook, if only to complain to the world about my lot.

There's a fellow I know, name of Mackenzie. He thinks we're friends. He means well, but the truth is that he's a really weird guy, and I've never been comfortable around him. Earlier today, I'd posted an update on Facebook, explaining that I had been hospitalized, and that I was experiencing a great deal of trauma, such that I had to request that nobody contact me.

I'd had a terrible afternoon. I just finished sitting in my own shit, until the hapless nurse arrived to clean me up – it's just humiliating. When she finished, I vomited, thereby setting off those gunshot seizures. I started crying in front of the nurse. And then my phone rang. Surely it must be my mother, calling in an emergency, as my friends knew not to bother me here.

It was Mackenzie. "Hey, Steve. How are you feeling?"

I got angry right away. " Mackenzie, have you read my Facebook post from today...?"

"Yes I did, but I needed to speak with you."

"No. I cannot talk now." And I hung up.

After a few minutes, my phone pinged, indicating an email. It was from Mackenzie. The subject heading read, "*I Know*". He went on: "*Not sorry i called. Just wanted you to hear my voice. Love you. Stay strong.*"

I knew I should have ignored him for my own good, but I replied:

But I AM sorry you called. I don't know how much clearer I could have been. The doctors are trying to save me, but they are discussing the possibility of this being my final days. My energy is scarce, and I need to reserve it for fighting these crazy side-effects. What energy I have left over goes to my family. The subject to your email says "I know"—but you DON'T know. Because if you did know, then you would understand to leave me in peace. Despite what you think, your phone call was not for me, it was for you. This is the second time you've done this, and it has to stop. Please do not even reply to this email.

Looking back, that may have been rather harsh, but I had to defend myself somehow.

Later that evening, a new nurse came into my room and asked me, without preamble: "Mr. Parton, did you urinate?"

Naturally, I replied with, "Yes I did. Uh, how about you?" Isabel was there, and she gave me the evil eye, but the nurse ignored me.

"And how much did you discharge?"

I thought about it. "Gee, I don't know."

She was undaunted. "Sir, I have to know."

So I made up a number. "Oh, I'm sorry. I peed 127 millilitres."

She looked at me askance. "Are you sure?" she asked. "That seems kind of low."

I decided to modify my carefully thought-out reply. "Whoops. It was actually 128 millilitres." She sighed, wrote down a number (or possibly a note about my behaviour), and trotted out of the room.

July 5

My room is the nearest one to the nursing station. As such, I can hear everything that goes on out there. The nurses are sometimes rather loud. In the wee hours of the morning, I asked Jana to close my door. When she asked why, I told her the nurses' voices were making it hard to sleep. She marched off to silence them but I called her back. I explained that my wife is a nurse who does nights, and one of the only things that keeps them all going through the whole night shift is the ability to gab to each other at the nursing station. Mind you, that same thing applies to the day shift as well. In any case, I told Jana that she only needed to close my door.

I asked Jana if my sweetheart, Esther, was working again tomorrow, but she said no. Esther was a matronly Jamaican lady who knew enough about medicine to make a doctor nervous.

"Who's working?" I asked.

"I don't know, but I'm the one who's doing up the schedule. So I'll make sure you have a good one."

"No, no," I replied. "There are other patients here who need one of the good nurses. Give me one of the grumpy ones. I can take it, and I'll turn her around." Jana nodded towards my roommate Bert, as my request was affecting the both of us. "Oh, he'll be fine," I said. "I'll deal with Bert."

I had a bit of a conundrum. I had previously committed to attending a concert tonight by The Redhill Valleys, the best alt-country band in Hamilton, at the Casbah nightclub. The thing was that the two beautiful women who front the band, Chelsea McWilliams and Danielle Beaudin, had invited me personally, which meant I was kind of obliged. (Truth be told, I am just in their fan group; it's not as if Chelsea called me up and said, "Steve, it's me. Are you coming to the show?") So, I asked the hospital if they could let me out to go to the night club. They said no, even after I explained what a fantastic band The Redhill Valleys is. I even posted a great idea on the band's fan page, proposing that they move the concert here to my hospital room. I was sure Brodie Schwendiman, the club's owner, wouldn't mind; he's always been a great guy. I just had to figure out how to get a sound system in here. In the end, I posted my regrets, and said I'd be thinking about them from my hospital bed.

Poor Alannah was one of my night time nurses. She was young and pretty, and really put up with a lot from me. No, I didn't try and flirt with her, even though Isabel wasn't there to threaten me with the evil eye. But when I found out her name was Alannah, I knew I would have to try to refrain from singing an Alannah

Myles song to her—and I love Alannah Myles. So I decided to be clever and instead say, "Are you tired of all the Alannah Myles references?" She rolled her eyes and said, "Yup." I said that I won't do that, to which she replied, "Yeah, you already did." That door was now open, so I had no choice but to sing to her as she moved on to tend to my roommate: "Black velvet, and that little boy smile..."

In the middle of the night, Alannah came into my room to give me my pain meds. I asked her if I could hold her hand. I explained that I'd had another attack, but it was in a new spot, and it was intense. I then felt a new attack coming on and, for some reason, I had the idea that it would be my last attack, accompanied by my last breath. So she held my hand and said some warm words of encouragement. It was hard to tell if she'd learned that from nursing school, or if she'd been reading all the comments on my Facebook posts: ("No, it's not your time, you've got this, etc.") But I gave the nurse a bit of a fright, thinking her patient might die on her while she held his damn hand.

Later that night, I needed a suppository, as I was bunged up yet again. Yvonne, one of the grumpy nurses, offered to give it to me, but I had no desire to let her get that intimate with me. I asked Alannah to do it. "Just be forewarned," I told her. "I have a super cute bum. I've been told a couple of times, by women, and by a couple of dudes."

She smiled. "Really?"

"No. Actually, my wife says my butt is not exactly like Burt Reynolds'. Oh, the envy."

July 6

I posted some news on Facebook:

You will never guess what amazing news I have to share (no, the tumours are still here). Last night, I had expressed remorse about my not being able to attend The Redhill Valleys' tour kick-off concert at the Casbah. I had suggested that they move the concert here to the hospital. The Casbah's owner, Brodie, jokingly replied that he would arrange for his liquor license to be transferred here for the night. But seriously, the show went on as scheduled, and I'm sure the performance was great. But today I got into a private discussion with Chelsea McWilliams and Danielle Beaudin from the band. They are coming to the hospital tomorrow to put on a mini concert here for me and a few of the other patients in the cancer ward. Damn-it, I'm crying as I write this. Man, I can't wait. People reading this, please go to: www.theredhillvalleys.com, download their CD and go see their shows—not just because they're a fantastic band, but because they have huge hearts. By the way, I tried to pay them for the show, but they'll have none of that. So instead, I'm making a donation to their next album, as they are

recording it with the smokin' hot Carl Jennings again. Ah,
somebody get me a Kleenex, fer cryin' out loud.

July 7

This afternoon I was asleep in my hospital room when I awoke
to find two beautiful women at the foot of my bed—holding
guitars! Danielle and Chelsea of The Redhill Valleys had arrived
to put on a private concert for a few of the patients and their
families and the staff of the cancer ward. But the concert was
actually for ME. Wearing my very un-cool hospital gown, I
showed Danielle and Chelsea to the common area of the ward,
with couches, jigsaw puzzles and a TV. Some of the patients
followed us in. My daughter was there as well, as she'd since
become a fan of the band's music.

Danielle and Chelsea asked me if I had any requests. Indeed,
there were a few of my favourite songs of theirs that I'd wanted,
and they played them. I also got to hear a couple of songs from
the new CD (we're all in for a treat, when it gets released).

I was quite drugged up, so I spent a good part of the show
tearing up at the beauty of the music. Then I would emerge and
start singing the male harmony vocal part out loud (Tim Allard,
the other member of the band, couldn't make it). So, I got to sing
with The Redhill Valleys—it's time to update my musical
résumé. I was so thankful for this private performance; it made
my entire week.

At 7:00 PM, it was time for the changing of the nursing shifts. All the nurses were out in the main area by the nursing station. Feeling strong, I grabbed my walker and shuffled out into the hallway, in front of all the nurses. Someone gave me a look, inquiring why I was out of my room, so I explained myself: "You can't have a party here without me." I received just enough chuckles to be emboldened, so I continued. "Esther, here's the problem with having you as a nurse—" Immediately everyone in the room stopped talking; the little pockets of conversation halted. Many people looked over at me, wondering where this was going to go. Esther was clearly the queen bee in the whole unit. I continued. "The problem was that I had you as my first nurse here, and now the bar has been set so high, that nobody can fill your shoes. Jana, Alannah, and Kelly, they gave it the ol' college try. But they're no Esther."

Then Nurse Marlene arrived on the scene, and said "Whatchoo doing here, out of your room?" I boldly put my arm around her. "And then there's Marlene, who's definitely in the top three nurses here." I was just trying to make people happy.

With Bert as my roommate, he and I spent a good deal of time talking. I learned that he was having a very rough time with life. He'd lost his driver's license and was on parole. He rents a room in a house with no visitors allowed, not even an occupational therapist or a personal support worker. A couple times a day, Bert would call people on his cell phone from his hospital bed, trying to reach folks who owe him money. It was all just sad. But he was proud that he hadn't had a drink or a smoke in the last three weeks. Coincidentally, he'd been here for three weeks, where he can't drink or smoke.

My family knew I couldn't handle having any more visitors (unless they played guitar and sang like birds). One fellow I know only from Facebook was quite adamant about coming to see me, and he contacted my sister Jenny. He pressed her for information about which hospital I was at, which unit and which room. He explained to Jenny that he and I have been close friends for many years, and that I'd requested his presence in my room. In fact, the guy is a self-proclaimed Social Justice Warrior and Conspiracy Theorist who often discusses the merits of beheading our country's leaders and dissidents. Understandably, he really freaks me out. I don't even know what he looks like, as his Facebook profile image only shows a picture of an Illuminati symbol. Thankfully, the guy's insincerity revealed itself to Jenny, and she declined to help him.

I learned that I would be going home that afternoon. Hearing this, Isabel said "I'm not sure where you're sleeping tonight, but I need you to know that, in the past week, I've gotten used to sleeping in the middle of our bed. So I don't know where you're going to sleep."

One of the nurses was talking about me, in front of me. She said, "Patient C-14 needs a walker before we can discharge him."

I was a little bit taken aback. "Hey," I said. "I have a name."

She apologized, and explained that the staff often referred to patients by their room and bed numbers for reasons of confidentiality. It made me think of the story of Dr. Patch Adams, who'd suggested that hospital staff should call patients by their names, instead of their numbers.

July 8

I was very happy to be home. After I settled in, Isabel showed me that crazy email I'd written back when I was waiting to be admitted to the hospital, and I was flabbergasted. My normally educated writing had gone to the dogs, with all the drugs I was on. But people who happened upon my words on Facebook were not privy to the fact that I was on large amounts of painkillers and was not myself. This became a problem during the last few days, as I had spent much of my time posting my thoughts on Facebook throughout my hospital stay. People responded to posts and comments that I don't remember writing. So if I've upset anyone, I'm sorry—somewhat sorry, anyway.

July 9

As we were getting ready to go to church, I took a double dose of my Oxycodone, as I was in a great deal of pain. While sitting in the pew, I became dizzy. The minster announced a song from their hymn book, and a voice rang out throughout the church: "Good God, not another song in A-flat!" Just then, the entire congregation turned to stare at me. "What?" I said. "Did I say that out loud?" Apparently, I did.

July 12

It's very nice to be home, and no longer in a hospital bed. During my stay, I continually wrote notes for this book. I'm just now doing basic editing with these notes. I was prolific, but my words were occasionally incoherent. Luckily most of it is still in my usually sharp memory. In this book, I tried very hard to avoid hyperbole – everything is written just as it happened, or just as I remembered it shortly after it happened.

I am part of the Dundas Writers Group. We meet once a month at a downtown pub. It's always a great time to stretch my brain. Most of the people there are smarter than I try to be. There are two PhDs among them. We discuss our writing: fiction, biographies, poetry and historical literature.

Last night I showed up at the meeting, though I should have stayed home. I was horrifically stoned, and I thought I was being very funny, telling bodily-function jokes from my hospital stay. Then I had a meltdown, and started to cry. It was all very embarrassing.

July 13

One of the hardest things to accept about cancer is that I am no longer a Tough Guy. Not that I was ever big and strong, looking for phonebooks to tear in half, but I used to be fit, and was afraid of nothing. Now I'm eighty pounds lighter than before cancer. I use a walker, and I can fall over with a good gust of wind. But I have a hard time accepting this fact, and I try to push myself. Seeing this, Isabel often offers to help me, to do things for me. And sometimes I feel emasculated, when she offers to carry something really heavy, like a glass of milk. Actually, the reason she prefers to carry my beverages is that I often spill them while in transit. It still makes me feel useless, though.

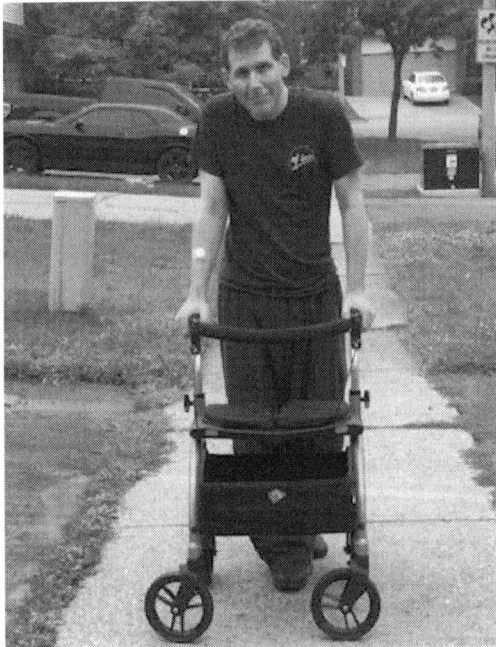

July 14

Last night I told Isabel that, if/when this cancer takes me, that I want her to find another man. After the words left my mouth, I was afraid that she'd spout off the names of a couple of fellows she thought would be right for the job. We had a bit of a cry then. But, of course, she simply replied that I will beat the cancer, and we'll grow old together. In writing this now, with a sober mind, I see that my words to her do not give her any credit for being a devoted partner. I need to stop writing, and go apologize to her. Be right back.

Long ago, when I survived my initial bout of cancer, I stopped shaking people's hands, and greeted everybody with a hug. "Handshakes are for strangers," I'd explain, when I wrapped my arms around someone who had held out a hand to me. Of late, I've been hugging everyone. I think even some of my gay friends may be saying, "Steve, give it a rest, man."

July 15

I found the sweet spot between pain and stonedness (wow, the spellchecker did not like that word at all). My pain is tolerable, and I have a medium buzz going on all day. I can't drive, but I can otherwise function. At least I have control of my brain. My mornings start off really slowly. I wake up, take my meds (waiting in a bottle beside my bed), and wait an hour for them to kick in.

July 16

Rick Spies, the minister at our church, had announced his retirement. In celebration of this, I'd composed a song for him. This morning, I performed it for him, in front of the congregation. In anticipation of my being unable to make it through the service, I took a double dose of pain meds that morning. Isabel was at work, so Sheelagh and Doug Wood picked me up to take me and my gear to the church. My friend Tomas was there, ready to accompany me on percussion. I set everything up and did a sound check, all with my walker. Then I sat in the front pew, waiting until it was my time to go up and play. When the time came, I had the idea that I didn't need my walker, and that I could simply stroll up to the chancel area, unaccompanied. I was wrong. Halfway between the first pew and the stairs to the chancel, my legs gave out and I tumbled to the floor. I heard a collective gasp, and the sound of shuffling as the men got up to rescue me. Tomas got to me first, and tried to lift me up. But I resisted. "Leave me be," I hollered throughout the sanctuary. "I just want to take a nap." Tomas and another man hauled me to my feet and up the stairs. They dumped me on my chair in front of the microphone and placed the guitar on my lap. Tomas prepared his percussion part. Reverend Rick finished introducing the song, and he gestured to us to begin. But I couldn't. "I don't know how to play guitar," I called out to him. Indeed, I had no idea what the first chord was or how the song was supposed to go. So instead, I turned the guitar over on my lap and talked to the congregation about the lyrical content. Then, without thinking about it, I just hit the first chord, and started playing. Everything else flowed the way it was supposed to. The lyrics rolled off my tongue and my fingers danced across the fret board.

After the song ended, Tomas helped me back down to my seat. Midway through the first prayer, I fell asleep in the pew. I tilted my head back, opened up my mouth and snored loudly. It's possible I may have embarrassed myself.

July 18

Things are levelling off, and I am now done with the intense painkillers. I have no more pills in my house, as I respectfully returned the leftovers to the pharmacy (this is because the street value for these is not as solid as it once was, and so I couldn't sell the remaining pills at Gore Park, downtown!)

Man, I just realized that there may be at least one knucklehead out there who may read my joke about hawking the pills, and not realize that I was kidding. So no, I didn't try to sell pills downtown.

July 20

Isabel and I saw The Doobie Brothers and Chicago tonight at the Budweiser Stage in Toronto (a few friends helped us out to make this happen). We sat in the handicapped section * sigh *.

Halfway through the Doobies' show, I couldn't sit anymore, so I stood up and danced. Yes I did (I leaned on the rail in front of me for support). Beside me, Isabel said, "Oh, no! What are you doing?" The thing is, when The Doobie Brothers are playing "Long Train Running," you can't not dance! By the second chorus ("*Without love—where would you be now...*"), I toppled over, into the arms of the guy behind me. Now, he and I are buddies for life, as evidenced by the photo below. I came to my senses and sat back down, but then, later, Chicago played "Feelin' Stronger Every Day." Gotta dance. I know I'm going to pay for it in the morning, and I can already feel the pain.

July 24

My first Cancer Trip book is finally available for sale on Amazon (paperback and eBook). Also, I'm on my third printing. To put things in perspective, JK Rowling does a bazillion books per printing, whereas I do 100. It's still very cool, though. The Amazon post took so long because I had had problems with them—a re-seller had taken over my book and decided to jack the price up to almost $50. I tried to reason with them. ("It's a 200-page dipshit memoir from an unknown author—nobody is going to pay fifty clams").

Finally, I threatened them with my wrath, and now it is back down to a reasonable price. Please check it out.

July 27

I sometimes feel badly for the ladies at the hospitals whose job it is to phone patients, setting up appointments. They must be bored, so it becomes my responsibility to liven their days up a little:

"Hello, Steve Parton? I'm calling to set an appointment with Dr. Slaven for next Wednesday at 10 AM."

"OoOoO, that's going to be a problem, I'm getting a new tattoo that day. Could you change it to Thursday?"

"Um, sir?" Then silence.

"Ah, I'm just kidding. Wednesday at ten it shall be."

July 31

I am not afraid of death. In fact, despite my prognosis, I spend all my time preparing to LIVE. I plan for tomorrow, next year, next decade. However, I'm a father. As such, I do need to acknowledge the possibility of my children not having me around much longer. I try very hard to show my daughter, Meghan, that she should have high expectations of how boys and men should treat her. But if I'm not around next year, who is going to teach my son Blake how to shave when he gets older? Or how to talk to girls? Or how to exercise good judgement when getting into a car full of teenagers? My friend Donna Mykytyshyn-Nunan suggested I shoot a series of short videos for my kids to watch when they get older. That's a great idea. I'll start them tomorrow.

August 3

The whole concept of social media networking is a fascinating one. I'm connected with a whole pile of people on Facebook. There are some friends, many acquaintances, and lots of people I've never met in the real world. Most times, when I post an update on my cancer battle, I receive a long barrage of comments, all wishing me well, giving me hope, and a reason to smile. But I never want people to feel obliged to comment; I sometimes go so far as to state that I don't need comments, that I'm just sending out an update.

I generally don't reply to the individual comments, as there are just too many. I guess I could copy and paste the word "thanks" under each one, but I usually just rest assured, knowing that the people assumed I read their posts, which I do. Sometimes I'll post a global thank you to everyone, but that's the best I can do.

Twice, however, people have called me on my Facebook response habits: "You know, Steve, I've left a few really nice comments on your posts, and you haven't replied to any of them. It's only common courtesy." Weird, eh?

Aug 9

At 3:25 AM I awoke to the sound of rain on the roof. It seemed like a good opportunity to go catch some Dundas night-life, so I went to sit outside on my front porch. One of those silly philosophical memes comes to mind: "Live each day like it was your last." Pshaw. When I was 17 my mother said, "Stephen, if you died tomorrow, you'd have lived a full life." To this I replied, "Yeah, but I ain't been laid yet, Ma." (okay, well I thought it, anyhow). I'm totally not ready to leave Isabel and the kids behind. But late-night, front-porch, rain-filled musings make for a good time to think about what I have been given. So many gifts. I have a car that runs. A house that's warm. A book collection. Children who love to read, and know how to ponder, and are kind to others. A different guitar for each genre of music. I have an electronic device that makes my guitar sound like I'm

75

playing through any amplifier in history. I've been shown more love than any human could withstand. My cat considers me his favourite person (well, in his top three, anyway). At 46, I can say that, if I died tomorrow, I'd have lived a full life. It's a beautiful night to die. Please let me go on a night like this, not on a stretcher, with tubes and probes attached to me.

Yesterday some poor bastard called me up to share cancer stories (it's a frequent occurrence, as my number gets passed around). This guy will be dead soon. Not because of his prognosis, but because he has no idea how to embrace the possibility of living. I had to cut him off and shut him out; he didn't want to hear my ideas. He said he was scared, and he was resentful over the fact that I am not scared.

I swear, I sometimes feel I could forgo all my meds and WILL this damn cancer away. My Victory Party is going to be awesome. I'm going to get drunk and say stupid shit (so, not a departure from my current *modus operandi*). There's going to be live music. I've actually started to write my short (not!) Thank-You speech. Somebody once suggested I write my good-bye speech for my funeral. Screw that. I'm writing my Victory Speech. So many thank-yous. I'll probably start by thanking Geddy Lee from Rush for his email to me. He's surely forgotten about me, but I haven't forgotten about him

Aug 10

I'm at the Juravinski Cancer Centre, in the chemo suite, awaiting my immunotherapy treatment. Someone just rang a bell, and the whole place erupted in applause, with hoots and hollers. It's my job to make sure I cheer more loudly than anyone. The bell is mounted on a plaque near the entranceway. It is to be rung by someone who has just had his/her final cancer treatment. I can't wait until it's my turn to ring that bell. One day.

In the meantime, I focus my energies on brightening the day for those around me, people who are also there to receive or administer treatments. I usually talk it up with the person on either side of my chair. And I sometimes get to have a short chat with the pretty raven-haired lady who empties the waste buckets in the unit. She calls me "yous guyses" even if I'm on my own. I love it.

The very first time I'd arrived here for my treatment, I asked the nurse if she knew how long it would take. She estimated it to be about an hour and a half. This surprised me. Although I'd had no experience here, no basis of comparison, I kind of thought it would all take around twenty minutes. I of course did not complain, not to the nurse, not to the ceiling. But a slight stream of exasperation must have slid across my face. I looked at the chair to my right, and the patient receiving his chemo was a young man in his twenties. He was asleep, and his mother sat by his side. She looked at me and said, ever so kindly, "My son comes here twice a week. And his infusion time is four hours." I dropped my jaw, and inwardly readjusted my attitude.

Isabel was at work, and I had to get to my school to teach guitar, or at least make sure the clocks were running on time. I was dizzy and dopey. I possessed just enough brain power to understand that it would have been dangerous to drive myself to work. So I trolled for a ride on Facebook. My request was posted as follows:

> *My fiends I can't dive my car I too drugged up it is not safe I did dropped of at my music school but I can not teach children so I cancelled there lessons. NO- it's THEIR lessons dumbass*
> *I had a ride home but he can't make is can I get a ride home from somebody I'm so sorry to dump this I think I had some bad spelling*
> *I will finished at my school at 7:30 can someone body pick me up I can take the bus but I might get lost*

Luckily for me, one of my "fiends" had a sense of humour, and I was given a ride to and from my school. Truth be told, I wasn't very productive that day. I spent most of my time hiding from the students' parents.

August 11

A very nice fellow enquired about buying my book, *Cancer Trip*. Although the book was available in some stores, he asked if he could just pick it up from my home, as he had some business to look after in Dundas. So I gave him my address, and he said he'd be right over.

Twenty minutes later, I had the cash in my pocket, and one less copy of the book on my shelf. The guy said he was excited to start reading it. It turns out he was so excited that he wanted to give me a report on his reading progress via email, after every dozen pages or so. Other than an initial reply of "Thank you very much; I'm glad you're enjoying it so far," I had to ignore the rest of his emails, as they kept coming and coming. I do still think he's a nice fellow.

August 15

I met with one of the nurse practitioners today. She is very good at her job, and seems to know everything. I happened to mention something about my victory party, that there will be booze, live music and dancing. I think I may have mentioned my plans to beat the cancer a time or two before, because the nurse rolled her eyes and said, "Look: you need to stop dreaming about your victory party; it's not going to happen. Start planning for the inevitable." So much for bedside manners. That really put a damper on my spirit. But I still had it in my mind that I was going to beat this thing. One of my strategies is to plan for success – not just in my mind, but through my actions.

August 19

My rock band, The Relics, performed on the main stage at the Dundas Cactus Festival. It was a beautiful Saturday afternoon, and a large crowd of people was there to hear us play. We brought out our A-game, throwing down Chicago, Rush and Supertramp. Halfway through the set, my spine (where the tumour is) flared up, and I started to experience killer pain. But this is rock 'n roll: I couldn't just slither off the stage in the middle of a show. Alan, our bassist, saw that I was in agony, so he came over to my area of the stage and stood right behind me, with his back against mine. He held me up so I could keep playing. When a guy says to another guy, "Brother, I've got your back", this is what he means.

Luckily for me, we were near the end of our show. As soon as we hit our final chord, I looked for Ted Kozack, side-stage. Ted has been a friend since school days, and he is our band's roadie. He was too far away for me to speak with him, but I just gave him a look that said, "I need you up here." Ted understood, and raced up the stairs, onto centre stage. He pulled my Fender Stratocaster off my shoulder, saying, "I got you, buddy." He carted me off the stage, down the stairs, my guitar in his other hand, then brought me to the back stage area and laid me gently on the grass. The guys in the band saw that I was in good hands with Ted, so they packed down my things as well as their own.

Within a few seconds of lying on the blessed grass, a lady came up to see if I was okay. She knelt down to tend to me.

"Waddaya need, dearie?" she asked.

I couldn't reply. The lady looked a bit familiar, but I couldn't place her face. Just then, Isabel arrived, and stepped towards me. But the lady beside me held up her hand. "Wait," she said to Isabel. "Steve's my Facebook friend. You need to know he has cancer."

Isabel smiled graciously, as she knew the woman was just trying to be helpful. But a spouse trumps a Facebook friend. Ted spoke up. He gestured to Isabel. "This is his wife."

I closed my eyes and decided to take a little nap, there on the grass. The band that was to follow us had arrived, and they had to walk around my still body as they carried their own gear from their truck to the stage. I heard one of them say to me, "Too much rock 'n roll, eh, man?"

August 23

It's high registration season at Avalon Music Academy. Even while getting my IV treatment at the chemo lab in the Juravinski, I still had to get to work, signing up music students. So I brought my laptop with me. Once the nurse inserted the IV needle and things were a go, I settled in and got to work. Really, I would have been doing the same thing at home. The difference was that here, I had nurses to fetch me cookies and juice. #LivingTheDream

August 24

Today, I was to have surgery on my spine, in the place where the tumour had caused havoc. After my last stay in the hospital, it was determined that one of my vertebrae, Lumbar 1, was collapsing. That was why I had back spasms. The vertebrae had been hollowed out. It had previously been filled by a cancerous tumour but the radiation killed the cancer, and left a big hole. I needed surgery. In fact, I needed two surgeries.

The first surgery was called Embolization. It was done to destroy excess blood vessels in and around the vertebrae that had been grown by the tumour. This would allow the Kyphoplasty to be done safely.

Isabel and I were up at 4:30 AM, as I had to check into the hospital by 6:00 for surgery. She dropped me off at the front doors, and drove off to park the car. At the pre-op reception, things looked bright, cheery and comfortable. The clerk smiled at me when I arrived at the counter and I handed her my health card.

"Good morning," she said. "What procedure are you having today?"

"Um, I have no idea."

"Really?" She cocked an eyebrow disdainfully. "You don't know what your operation is?"

"Well, it's got a fancy name. I can't, uh, I don't know. Why don't you surprise me?"

"Okay, then. Gender Reassignment Surgery, it shall be. Please sign these forms."

She grinned as I defensively grabbed my crotch, and my memory instantly sprang to life. "It's for my spine! I think it's called Hyper plasticine." Just then, my wife arrived and started towards me. "Isabel! Tell the lady I don't want to become a woman!"

Isabel just asked, "What have you done, now?"

The receptionist turned to her. "Please tell me the name of the procedure we're to be performing on your husband."

"It's Kyphoplasty."

"Wonderful. Please have a seat."

I came back to the conversation and turned to the receptionist. "You mean you knew all along what I'm having?"

"Of course. We don't negotiate these things on the spot; we don't ask what kind of surgery you would like to have." She nodded to her computer screen. "It's stated here, right next to your name. But we always confirm with the patient."

Soon, I was brought into the pre-op area, where patients are kept until the OR is ready for them. A nurse arrived and drew the curtain so I could have some privacy while changing into my hospital gown. Isabel was inside there with me, and I motioned to her while I said to the nurse, "I don't know who this lady is; we met in the lobby downstairs." The nurse didn't believe me, so she replied, "Well, that's a good way to get to know each other. See you in a few minutes."

As far as surgeries go, this one was relatively minor. I was put under and, after the perceived one-second passage of time, I awoke in Recovery. It was an enormous room, maybe forty beds. Shortly after, Isabel arrived (bucking the rules) and gave me my cell phone. After my new nurse got me settled and did my vitals, I was left alone. Having been awake since 4:30 AM, I fell fast asleep.

Soon, my cell phone rang, waking me up, so I answered it. This turned out to be a colossal mistake, as my mind was still under the influence of the drugs given to me before the surgery.

There was a lady on the other line, and the conversation went thus:

"Uhhh, hullo...?"

"I think I have the wrong, um, is this Avalon Music Academy...?"

My mind searched for a reply. I knew this. I gave the best answer I could come up with: "I think so." I was awesome.

"You think so? I believe I have the wrong number."

"No! Wait. I own a music school. It's called... wait, I can do this. Shit. What did you say it was called again?"

"Now I know I have the wrong number. Good bye."

She hung up. Immediately, my cell rang again. Logic fought for supremacy in my mind as I knew I shouldn't touch the phone. But I had answered at least half the questions right on the previous try, so this one would of course be much better. I always answer the phone by stating the name of my school.

"Hello, um, Avalon-something. Damnit."

It was the same lady. "You still haven't figured out the name of your school yet, have you? The thing is, I checked the number, and this is correct, so I don't know what's going on."

I figured I'd start by telling her what I knew. "I own the music school. I just had surgery. I had a general Anastasia and I'm in the recovery room." To prove it to her, I came very close to telling her I had a catheter in, and that it really hurt, but a thought came to my brain: "Steve, don't be an idiot: she won't know what a catheter does to you, as she's not a guy. Just tell her your penis hurts."

Before I could say anything, she continued. "I'm clearly calling your cell phone."

Then it hit me, and a bit of the cloud lifted. "The school line sometimes goes to my cell. Before the surgery, one of our music teachers was supposed to change that. I guess he forgot. Not gonna name names, but it rhymes with 'Shrebilcock.'"

"Okay. Anyway, I'll try you back in a few days."

I'd posted the above story on Facebook, tagging the teacher, Mike Trebilcock. His reply: "'Rhymes with 'Shrebilcock'? Well, that could be anybody.'"

Later on, when my brain began to come close to being fully functional, I checked my call display and called the lady back. I apologized, and she was very understanding. In the end, she signed up her two daughters for music lessons. Yup. I still got it.

After a short while, I was moved from Recovery into one of the units, where I was to spend the next day and a half, until I was well enough to leave. Isabel was shocked when she saw me there. I was completely covered in monitoring devices, oxygen tubing, etc. After a time, the devices were removed, one by one. Isabel, seeing that I was looked after, went home.

Towards evening, my bed was given to another patient, and I was given a chair in which to sleep. This wasn't because I'd drawn the short straw. Truth be told, the hospital bed shortage in

Hamilton is a sad reality. After hearing the nurses explain several times on the phone that they had no available beds, I told my nurse to give my bed to someone else. Here's the thing: A few hours ago, I had been in recovery, just following my surgery, feeling like a bag of dirt. I was extremely uncomfortable. But I was in a bed. I heard that the latest patient was waiting for a bed while sitting in a damn chair. I'd had enough. I spoke to my nurse, and she helped me into a chair, where I sat by myself in the corner of the room. She was very thankful. Isabel explained to me later that a patient coming out of surgery would never be put in a chair, but I didn't know that.

Shortly, a new patient was wheeled into the unit and given my old bed. All of a sudden, I realized just how hard and uncomfortable my chair was. On the bright side, I had a place to put my water, and I had my own private hand sanitizer dispenser nearby. The nurse returned and gave me a blanket, telling me that I would hopefully get my own bed before the night was through.

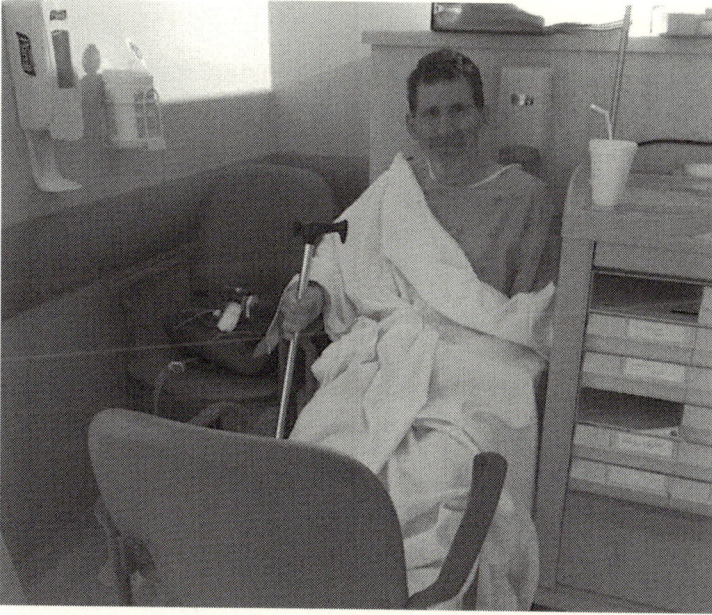

I drifted off to sleep, but only briefly. My bum started to hurt, and I began to question my eternal quest to be a nice guy, as I thought about spending the entire night in that chair. I looked over at the other patient, lying snug-as-a-bug in my bed. I had considered trotting over to him and shaking his shoulder, saying "Hi. Sorry to wake you. That's actually my bed, but I gave it up, to be a nice guy. Only now I've changed my mind. So maybe I can have the bed back, and you can take a turn in that chair over there. It's quite comfortable – lovely, really."

The nurse returned, this time with a pillow. I fell asleep again, but was soon woken up with the news that I was to be moved to a new bed in another ward. I was told that the nurses there had more patients to attend to than in the previous ward, so

I would receive considerably less attention. But that didn't matter, as it was night time.

But talk about karma: whereas I was previously in a ward with about twenty other patients, my new room had only one other bed. My roommate, Chester, was fast asleep. He was an old fella, and I learned that he was mute. By comparison, my former ward was a very loud place. Sometimes we make our own luck.

At 2:45 AM, I woke up again. I think I may have been too smug after moving to this room. My roommate, the nice, quiet old man, just had his diaper changed. I figured the best course of action would have been to have my nose removed. I was dying there, and I actually thought about asking for my chair back in the other ward. I guess Karma doesn't apply to those who are smug.

August 25

When I woke up in the morning, Mandy, my nurse, had to ask me some skill-testing questions, to make sure I was cognisant. She lobbed me a couple of softballs: "What's your name?" (Steve) and "What country are you in, now?" (Canada). Then the questions became harder: "Who's our Prime Minister?" All I could think to say was, "The young guy. Pierre Trudeau's kid."

She gently placed her hand on my forehead for a couple of moments. Her touch was soft and warm, and it made me happy.

Just then, Isabel arrived, and I felt like I had been unfaithful to her, the way the nurse was touching my forehead.

Mandy smiled and left the room. Isabel looked at me strangely. "What's wrong?" she asked.

"The nurse. I think she wants me."

Isabel rolled her eyes. "Does she, now?"

"Well, I only date nurses. You know that."

"That's it," she said. "I'm taking a photo of you, for you to look at. You know that I love you, but have you seen yourself lately? Right now, you're a bit of a mess. And besides, we're not dating; we're married."

"Really? That's awesome." I glanced down at Isabel's ring finger and saw a couple of rings that I'd put on her years ago.

After my lunch, Mandy came in to tend to me, and ask me a couple more trivia questions. "What city are we in, now?"

I answered excitedly. "Hammer Town!"

"Pardon me?" she asked.

I explained that The Hammer was Hamilton's nickname. "Please ask me some harder questions."

She ignored me, and pulled a pen from her pocket. "What does this do?"

Two possible replies came to mind: (A) "It's used to stab people in the eye who ask stupid-ass questions", or (B) "It writes on paper." I went with (B).

"Good, Stephen." She smiled. "Now, what year is this?"

91

"It's 2017. Please ask me something harder than kindergarten level."

"Well, we have to ask cognitive questions. Why don't you give me an example?"

I thought for a moment, and then said, "What were the first four provinces in the initial Dominion of Canada in 1867?"

Mandy ignored me, and felt my foot for a pulse. There were blue marker circles all over it. I had an idea, so I pointed to my foot and said, "Those circles were put there by a certain impressionist artist from New York, popular in the 60's and 70's. What's his name?"

She looked away for a moment. "You mean Andy Worhol?

"Yes. Now, that's a cognitive question you could have asked."

It wasn't much longer before they sent me home. Mandy was probably happy to see me go.

August 27

The surgery was a success, and I recuperated. After a couple of days, I had to get back to focusing on work. I had three job interviews to conduct, for new music teachers. The first two were easy. Aleef and Jackson were both former guitar students at our school, and I'd already decided to hire them. But it was still necessary to do a formal interview. In turn, each of the two young men showed up at my house, and was directed to my bedroom. I was sitting up in my bed, surrounded by pill bottles, and an empty pee bottle. The guys didn't bat an eye, but answered my questions with conviction. I hired them both. The only problem with Aleef and Jackson was the fact that they are likely better guitar players than I am!

For the third interview, a young lady was also scheduled to come to my home and interview for the job of flute teacher. I knew I couldn't invite her up to my bedroom, so I braved the staircase and set myself up on the couch to receive her.

Two minutes before she was due to arrive, my cell phone rang. It was a mom inquiring after flute lessons. The mom and I were in the middle of a nice chat when the doorbell rang. Isabel greeted the new prospective flute teacher and led her into our living room. I smiled and indicated that I would not be long on the phone. Just as we were about to wrap up the conversation, the mom asked me the name of the flute teacher. I put my hand over the phone and leaned towards the girl sitting beside me on the couch.

I whispered, "What's your name, again?"

"Becky."

I returned to my phone call. "The teacher's name is Becky."

Next, I needed to make sure this girl was right for the job.

August 31

A couple of weeks ago, I asked Shoppers Drug Mart for a refill of one of my opioid prescriptions. I'd noticed that the doctor who wrote the original script was an unfamiliar doctor, and was from

Urgent Care (this is a place that's sort of a cross between a walk-in clinic and an Emergency Room). I knew that Urgent Care never renews scripts for anybody, particularly when the drug is a narcotic. So I told the pharmacy assistant to ask my own doctor for the renewal, and not to ask Urgent Care. Then I forgot about it.

At 10 PM a few days later, my phone rang, waking me up. It was a lady from Urgent Care, and she was yelling at me. Apparently, the pharmacy had accidentally contacted them for my refill, and the lady there was angry about it. I tried to explain that it wasn't my fault, but she yelled some more, then hung up on me. I didn't get her name, but I called back the next day, and asked to speak with the administrator, the boss of Urgent Care. I told her what had happened, and she knew exactly who I was calling about.

"Do you wish to make a formal complaint?" she asked.

"No, I'm calling because the angry lady probably just needs a hug."

I heard the boss chuckle. "Well, she's not the huggable type. But I'll talk to her."

That was good enough for me.

September 5

On the first day of music lessons, my school was flooded with students and their parents. There were people from last year, as well as new folks. I greeted one lady who was there with her two daughters, and her voice sounded familiar. I asked her a question quietly, so no one else could here: "Say, when you signed your kids up for music lessons over the phone, was I really stoned?"

She smiled. "I remember that. And yes you were."

"Cool," I said. "I already wrote about it in my new book. I hope that's okay."

September 12

I am so blessed to be in my position. I have a good number of friends to help me out when I need it. And I also have Facebook friends, people I don't know in real life, but who will answer the call when I need something.

At 2:00 in the morning, I realized that I was in need of a ride for the following day. Isabel was on nights, and I had to go see a doctor. So I posted a request on Facebook for a ride. Thirty seconds later, my phone pinged, as someone I hadn't met before offered to help. The arrangements were made, and I went back to sleep, knowing that all was right with the world.

September 15

In *Cancer Trip Book 1*, I made it quite clear that I'd been taking cannabis as a cure for cancer. One problem that arose was in the way so many people wanted to welcome me into their culture of pot. Don't get me wrong, I love hippy music – The Grateful Dead, The Doors, The Byrds, etc. But I wanted nothing to do with the marijuana lifestyle. I never smoked my pot; I distilled it into oil, and took daily capsules. My house has no bongs, or posters of Bob Marley or Cheech and Chong. One day, I was offered the loan of a book by a very friendly young man I'd never met. He told me I'd LOVE the book, and he even offered to bring it over to my house. I replied that I already have a line up of books waiting to be read. Furthermore, I'd probably lose his book, and then have to buy him a new one when he asked for it back – even though I didn't want it in the first place. So he decided he would just give it to me. I tried again to decline, but he brought it to me anyway. The book had plagiarized some well-known cartoon characters from my childhood, and depicted them all smoking pot. It was weird.

Later on, Isabel saw the book on the living room table, and suggested we give it to my one-year-old nephew as a gift. Then she looked at it a little more closely, and saw that the cartoon character had a big honking joint in his mouth. It was no longer a book for children.

September 18

I don't know what the hell I'm smiling for. I had had this idea that if I willed hard enough to see NED (No Evidence of Disease) on my CAT scan result today, it would just happen. But in fact, the cancer has now spread through my lungs. I asked how many tumours there are, and Dr. Hotte just said "Lots. They

96

didn't count them all". I'm so sick of this shit. It looks like I'll have to put off my Victory Party for a while yet.

They are going to start me on a new experimental drug. I'm going back to the Juravinski tomorrow, and I'll find out more about the next game plan.

September 19

Earlier in the year I'd tried an immunotherapy for a few months, but the doctors determined that it wasn't working for me. This time, they were going to try the same treatment, only pairing it with an additive that had recently shown some promise. To receive the drug, I had to agree to take part in a clinical trial, which I've always been fine with. This was a Phase 2 trial. As part of the process, the drug makers have to disclose their findings from the previous testing. There were actually two versions of the additive. In Phase 1, they'd tested Additive A on 29 people, two of whom died as a result of the drug. But Additive B had shown some really promising results. The patients are randomly selected to decide who gets which drug. I decided I'd prefer to receive the version that doesn't kill people, but the decision was out of my hands. It was explained to me that a computer will randomly select the drug for me. I was a little anxious about which one I would receive.

September 28

Isabel and I flew with the kids out to Vancouver to visit friends and family. The trip was hampered somewhat by the fact that my spine started acting up again. In the airport, Izzy and the kids carried my luggage. It felt good to have my hands free, but I was embarrassed that I couldn't pull my weight. The only thing that almost got us into trouble was when, in the area where our carry-on bags were being scanned, Meghan announced out loud that there were no B-O-M-Bs in our bags. When I gave her the evil eye, she whispered, "I knew we couldn't say the word 'bomb', so I spelled it."

In the end, it was a successful trip, visiting family and friends, riding the ferry boat over to the island and going on a whale-watching trip.

October 5

I screwed up my meds, and now I'm paying the price for it, as I am very ill. I had had some dipshit little pill that was supposed to combat side effects of the other pills, to protect my stomach. I was starting to wean off of it, but I forgot to put it in my arsenal of meds, so I essentially stopped cold turkey. Whoops. According to the pill-maker's website: "*If you stop taking these tablets suddenly, you may experience unpleasant side effects including sweating, shaking, worsening of angina, irregular heartbeat, heart attack or death. Withdrawal should be gradual.*" Awesome. I'm off to the hospital now. When they ask the reason for my visit, I'll just state, "Because I'm stupid." Actually, I have a bunch of tests to do today, so I'm there anyway. The adventure continues.

I did secure some more pills, and I restarted the regimen. Things were fine after that.

October 10

At 3:30 AM, it occurred to me that my bucket list has not been completed—despite the time I boasted otherwise, perhaps with an air of pompousness. I've never ridden a Triumph Bonneville T100. It's my favourite motorcycle, and I always point them out to Isabel, whenever we see one. To be honest, I've never driven a motorcycle; I've only ridden on the back a few times. In this day and age, I hope I don't have to relinquish my man card for riding on the back of a bike. So I turned to Facebook to see if there was anyone who had this motorcycle, a sense of humour, and who wouldn't mind letting me ride on the back for fifteen minutes.

Wayne Hodgson is a biker who grew up in Dundas. He and I have lots of mutual friends, but we hadn't met before. And he rides a Triumph motorcycle. He heard about my request through my friend, Linda Mykytyshyn, and he called me up with an offer I couldn't refuse (see the next entry).

October 13

Whenever the 13th of the month falls on a Friday, huge numbers of bikers converge on the town of Port Dover for a massive party. Wayne had plans to attend, but he stopped by my house on the way down, riding a brand new Triumph Bonneville T-120, on loan by his buddies at Sturguss Cycle. He offered to take me on the Triumph all the way down to Port Dover – and I so wanted to go. But it was a bad day. I was in so much pain, I knew it wasn't going to happen. I settled for taking some photos of that gorgeous machine in our driveway. (On the flipside, Wayne has since become a really good friend. He lives up North, and checks in on me regularly).

October 20

I watched the documentary on CTV about the beloved Canadian rock band, The Tragically Hip. Gord Downie, the singer, was diagnosed with terminal brain cancer, yet he continued to tour with the band. It was incredible. I'm now embarrassed for all the times people have called me brave for the way I continue on living and performing music despite my illness. I am not brave, I am not strong—Gord Downie was these things. The man was a force of nature, so deserving of all the praise across this country.

October 21

Hmm. Earlier this evening, while watching the Tragically Hip documentary on CTV, I opined about our lots (Gord Downie's and my own). I'll readjust my sentiment herein to state simply that I understand what Gord went through on stage, if on a smaller scale. What we have in common is band mates (in my case, Alan Hinckley, Michael Scott and Steve McRae) who completely understand what we're dealing with, and provide huge support and love. The same goes for our crew, Ted Kozack. Where I differ from Gord (outside of the obvious) is that my audiences usually don't know that I'm sick. Sometimes it may appear that I've had too much to drink, when in fact I'm literally willing myself not to die before the end of the show. Isabel, in the audience, my nurse/wife who comes on tour with my band, can read my face during these moments. My band mates can feel it as well, as my playing is not very good during these episodes. But when people hit the dance floor right in front of our stage, or request a Rush song because they know we can pull it off, it's all worth it. Often, during the ride home (with Ted behind the wheel), I proclaim to myself that that was my last gig. Even my loving family has proposed that I stop performing, because of the toll it takes. But I can't stop. Then the cancer would win already. And I'd be heartbroken. I get a lot of joy seeing fellow musician Annette Haas post all her shows on Facebook. Really, she's the hardest-working musician in Hamilton, in my opinion. But if I didn't have my own gigs to go to, then each of Annette's posts would be a reminder that I'd have given up. And that just won't do.

October 25

I had to post on Facebook for help again:

Does anyone want to do a sleepover at my place tonight? I'm pretty sure I'm going to have a rotten night, and I just need someone to be around, in case I need help. We have a nice guest room. I'll probably watch a rerun of "Better Call Saul", and then hit the sack. The last time I trolled Facebook for someone to sleep here with me, I was adamant that it be a male, as I didn't want a lady to see my tears, I needed someone strong enough to perhaps haul me off my bed and, lastly, there are the optics with my wife, who often works nights. Luckily, she still loves me. In any case, I'm fine with having anyone here—as long as you are someone I know well. Please bring your own entertainment, as I'm not at my best these days. Lastly, don't ask my friend Cam for a reference, as he had a bit of an unpleasant time at my place last year—but it was a unique experience, to be sure.

My friend John Hall and I had gone to school together when we were children. He was well liked, happy to be friends with everyone. He lives just down the street from me, and he answered the call when he saw my post asking for help.

John and I hung out for a while in the evening, then he went to the spare room and I went to mine. At around 2 AM, I felt like I was going to be sick. I called out for John, and he came running in. After emptying my belly into the toilet, I was unable to move, so he brought me a pillow where I lay, on the bathroom floor. John sat with me on the floor and inevitably the stories started up again and so did the laughter. 2 AM on the bathroom floor – that seemed like a great time for a selfie.

October 26

One of the stipulations for my present clinical trial was that I had to undergo several base-line tests, prior to starting. Among them was a biopsy on my lungs, which involved removing several small samples of the tumours.

The doctor and nurses were great, considering what an awful ordeal it was for me. The procedure was complicated by the fact that lying down flat on that board was brutal for my spine. All tests, scans, MRIs, etc. required me to be on my back for the next four months of procedures. It was torture.

After the biopsy was all finished, I asked one of the nurses to take a photo of me holding the tumour biopsies (in a bag). She actually rolled her eyes when I told her it was for Facebook, saying "Are you sure you want to do that?" But I did, and I posted the photo as soon as I arrived home.

Some people thought it was funny or interesting, but one person unfriended me as a result. He was adult enough to message me, explaining that he does not need to see my TMI (Too Much Information) posts. I know this person in real life, and he's a good man. I respect him very much for bringing this to my attention, which then begged the question: are my posts TMI? Do I need to back off a little (or a lot)? It's actually been very helpful for me, sharing my journey on Facebook, and receiving loads of support.

I chatted with the fellow who had unfriended me, and I thanked him for his message and his candour. We discussed the possibility that others may feel this way. To give him his due, he's a cancer survivor, and he stated that my posts gave him a constant reminder about his own battle with the disease. We're all good.

October 27

Another rant for Facebook:

Some people call me brave or strong, as my Facebook posts are always positive, in the face of my impending doom.

105

That's going to change, if only for this very post. You've been warned. Feel free to scroll away, unfriend, or unfollow. Moving on. I rescind my post of last night in which I apologized for my use of TMI on Facebook. I've decided I don't give a shit. You know how to break the connection. Below, find my next TMI post. It's a doozy.

Yesterday I had a biopsy on my lungs. They stuck a rod through my back, extracted a piece of a tumour from my lung, and repeated that six more times. It's as unfun as it sounds. Today, I can't pee, as the procedure did something to my bladder. You know that feeling when you have to pee so badly it hurts? I've been experiencing that since 5:00 this morning. I'm probably going into Emerg for the day.

So here's some honesty for which you signed up, if you are still here: today is an awful day so far. On top of everything else, I've been vomiting. I'm still dealing with the effects of tumours in my spine. You haven't experienced this level of pain until you try worshipping at the porcelain altar and, during each retch, someone smashes your back with a baseball bat. In my haze, I actually looked behind me, to see if Joey Bautista was there with his bat. I've been calling out loud to die, as I'm finished now. I don't want to continue like this (to be honest, I'm not so foolish as to actually take my own life—I would never do that). But I'm just saying I would invite a release to all this. Even Isabel finds it trying, waking up to my late-night screaming.

A nurse from VON came over to collect a sample of urine, directly from my bladder. My abdomen was in pain, and I couldn't pee. And can you guess from which orifice the instrument entered my body. It was a horrible time. I'm now in the hospital again. I'm not sure when I'm getting out.

There is another reason why I have such resentment for cigarette smokers (besides the stench). It's that they are knowingly sending themselves to a life that parallels my own. If you could see me on one of my bad days, I'm sure you would quit cold turkey. But don't worry, everyone; tomorrow I'll probably be back to my brave smiley-face photos.

October 28

In the hospital, they did tests on my bladder and spine. It turned out there was no problem with my bladder. We never found out why I had belly pain, but it eventually went away.

Thank you, everyone, for the support and the kind words. The past two days were extremely rough since the lung biopsy. Now it's 5:30am, and I've been up since 1:00. I know I can't reply directly to all the kind comments left on my posts, but please know that I read and enjoyed all of them. I've cleared my whole weekend so I can recover. It broke my heart to have to cancel a recording session with the amazingly talented Charlene Henry, but it was for the best.

It's all about the small victories: I went 26 hours with no food, and I've broken my fast with pudding. It was mostly good (more on that later). Lots of tests, and they still don't know for certain why my spine is giving me so much grief. Nevertheless, my symptoms have started to abate, so I'm going home soon. It's been a very rough journey. Last night, Isabel and I got home from the Juravinski Cancer Centre at 6pm. She went to fetch me some water, and she dropped the glass, which smashed onto the kitchen floor. So she sat down and had a good cry. Make no mistake; this disease is just as hard on the partner as it is on the patient. Now, on to the complaining: the pudding would be great except that it has granola and cinnamon in it! Who the hell does that? Jeez, no wonder people complain about hospital food! Well, the doctors and nurses were great, as were the ambulance techs who took me to the Juravinsky, so I guess there's that.

October 29

A few weeks ago, at the end of my appointment with Dr. Kapoor, he asked me if I liked the band Guns 'n Roses. Of course I do. He told me they were coming to Toronto, and that we should go see them together. That sounded like a great idea. We almost convinced Dr. Hotte to come with us, but he wasn't able to make it. So it was just Dr. K and me. We drove to Toronto in his fancy sports car, and talked about things unrelated to kidney cancer. The concert was great, and we ran into many people we knew there. And, once we got back to Hamilton, Dr.

Kapoor went in to the hospital to perform emergency surgery at 1:00 in the morning.

October 31

My appointments with my oncologist, Dr. Hotte at the Juravinski Cancer Center, are usually every three weeks or so. This year, luck was on my side, as I was given an appointment for October 31st. Fellows my age don't get many chances to wear a Hallowe'en costume, but there was no way I was going to pass on the opportunity to wear something scary to the doctor's appointment. I decided I didn't want to risk being the only person in the entire hospital in a costume. So when the nice lady called to confirm my appointment the week before, I told her she needed to promise that Dr. Hotte would be wearing a costume as well—otherwise, I wouldn't be going. The poor lady said she would try to pass on the message, but that she couldn't guarantee the doctor would actually dress up.

When Hallowe'en arrived, naturally, I wore my prized Darth Vader outfit. At the cancer clinic, I usually begin by getting my blood taken. The ladies drawing blood were amused at my appearance. I rolled up a sleeve, but kept my mask on. Isabel took a photo of me and the tech. I turned away from the tech, and explained that the needle hurts less if I look away. I then posted the photo to the Internet, where it immediately became a meme.

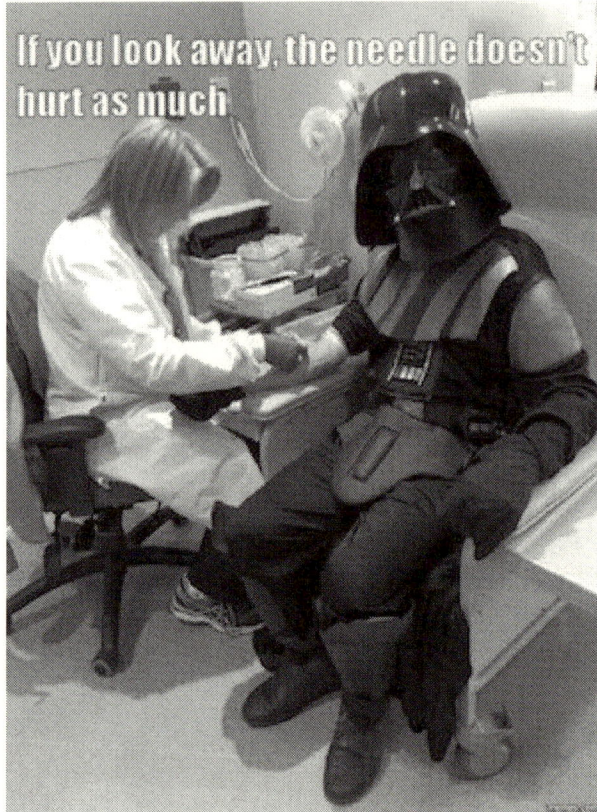

If you look away, the needle doesn't hurt as much

Shortly after, I checked into the doctor's waiting area, where I was by now well-known to the staff. The lady behind the counter said she needed to see my health card—and my face (as the mask covered my whole head). Breathing heavily, electronically, like the *Star Wars* character I was dressed as, I waved my hand at her, and used The Force: "You do not need to see my face." But she was immune to my attempt at magic. "Yes, I do," she said. "And your card." Darth Vader had no pockets, so neither did I, since I was wearing his clothes and all. The solution had been to have Isabel carry my wallet, phone and some snacks. She's awesome, that way. She produced my health card and I lifted up my mask, letting the lady have a glimpse of my grinning face. "Thaaank you. Please have a seat." The receptionist turned to the next person in line.

I started to explain that Darth Vader waits for no one, but Isabel grabbed my arm and guided me to a chair. "Here, Darth, I brought you the funny pages, and a granola bar." I resolved myself to my wait, and read the paper, a difficult task with my mask on. When the health care aide came out and called for "Steve Parton," I explained that I no longer go by that name, and that I should be referred to as Lord Vader, the Dark Lord of the Sith. "Of course," she said. "You'll be in Room Six, uh, Lord Vader."

I can't remember much about the appointment, what we talked about, other than the fact that I still have cancer. Shoot. But I do remember that Dr. Hotte didn't disappoint me, as he was wearing a costume of his own (some silly hat), per my earlier request. It wasn't as spectacular as my *Star Wars* bad guy outfit, but it at least led to a photo-op.

Back home, I spoke to Isabel as if she were one of my arch enemies from the rebellion: "Don't defy me, or I shall have to use

The Force on you." Strangely, Isabel showed no fear. I waved my lightsaber around the living room, to show that I meant business. Unfortunately, it was a fake lightsaber, which meant that, although it was effective at scaring the cats, it would not inflict any damage on an opponent—or the furniture.

Later that afternoon, I went to pick up my kids from elementary school. Of course, I wore my Darth Vader costume for this venture. I still hadn't taken it off since the doctor's appointment. When I arrived in front of the building to wait with all the other parents for the children to emerge, I received a few looks of concern. Nobody was frightened of my character; rather, they were unhappy about a person in a face-hiding costume, stalking outside a school. So I marched in the front door and presented myself to the secretary:

"Afternoon, Linda."

"Oh, hi, Steve".

The best part was when my daughter emerged, took one look at Darth Vader and said, "Hi, Daddy." She took my hand and we walked to the car.

And, yes, I wore my costume to my school that day to teach guitar lessons. All of that made for a great Hallowe'en.

November 10

Today I took my third ambulance ride this year. My daughter Maggie was home, and she witnessed me having a horrific back spasm, screaming out loud. The vertebrae (near where the miserable tumour is) acted up again, and I couldn't move when I woke up. There were two problems: I had to cancel a much-anticipated jam session with some old friends. And, also, there was a fear of losing all movement below the belt. The hard part was letting down my musician friends.

Maggie got to dial 911, something she's always wanted to do. But, to her dismay, she didn't get to ride in the back of the ambulance.

November 19

The tumour in my spine continued to do some damage. So I had to have Kyphoplasty surgery again. Like the last time, they had to fill another one of my vertebrae with rubber cement.

Due to my history with surgeries, I knew I would wake up with a brain that didn't fully function. This time, I came out of my anaesthesia next to a fellow my age who had also just emerged. The nurses were busy, so I addressed my new friend. He was just as loopy as I was. We talked nonsense for a full fifteen minutes until a nurse came to check my vitals. The other patient asked me what I'd had done, so I replied the best way I could: "I have no idea."

He then changed the topic. "Did you see the Steelers game?"

I had to think about it. "What sport is that, again?"

"Uh, I can't remember. I think it's hockey. But it might be football. I love football. I use to play pro."

"Really?"

"No."

"Well, I missed the game. But I watched *Frozen* with my daughter. Again. I know all the songs in the movie." Then I had an idea, "Do you want me to sing one?"

"Of course."

That was when a porter arrived to take me to a ward, where I would remain for the next few hours. It was a good thing for me, as it would have been foolish to try and sing "Let It Go", at least not without a good vocal warm up.

Dr. Drew, the surgeon who had done my procedure, found Isabel in the waiting room. He explained to her: "The surgery was a success. Your husband is in recovery, chatting up all the nurses, even the ones not assigned to his bed."

In the ward, I introduced myself to the old man in the bed next to me, who replied that his name was Harold. The man soon fell asleep, and he filled the entire ward with The Snore To End All Snores. I started to get worried about the coming night, and how difficult it would be to sleep next to this guy – but he was released within the hour. Harold: The Friend I Never Knew.

I was wearing my hospital gown, the one that allows a patient's butt to hang out. I climbed out of bed, leaned on my cane and stood there, looking down the ward to see if the washroom was free. A nurse wearing green scrubs asked if she could help me.

"No thanks," I replied. "I'm just heading downtown to go dancing."

The nurse became upset. "No you're not!"

I smiled to myself, then I realized that she must have thought I was a mental patient trying to escape. (This ward had all manner of patients). I trotted towards the washroom, and she let me be. Later that day, two other patients had tried to leave. I heard a nurse ask an elderly man where he was trying to go. He replied that he was off to catch the bus. Another time, a patient asked the nursing station, "Do you know what time the next train to Windsor is?"

After Harold had left, his bed was occupied by an elderly lady, name of Mrs. Bull. Through the curtain that separated our beds, I heard Mrs. Bull call out for her nurse. Her voice was feeble, and surely could not be heard beyond my bed. So I called out through the curtain. "Ma'am? Just hit the red button on the chord. Then the nurse will come over."

Mrs. Bull replied that she couldn't find it. "Would you like me to go over there and find it for you?" I asked.

"Yes, please"

"Okay, it'll only take me a minute. I just have to unhook a couple of tubes and pretend it doesn't hurt like the dickens to walk. I'm on my way. Do you have to go to the WC?" (I'm reasonably fluent in Senior-speak. WC stands for Water Closet, an old-timey word for the washroom.)

I made my way over to her bed, but I couldn't find her call button. I traced the chord from the wall plate, and discovered that the switch was underneath her bum. I decided that my investigation was now over. "Ma'am, I can't find it. I'll just go get the nurse."

The nurse was at her station, and she came right away. "What can I get for you?"

I heard Mrs. Bull reply, "My favourite colour is orange. Not many people give orange enough of a chance." The nurse, to her credit, told the lady that orange was HER favourite colour, too. I could hear the patient smile through the curtain. As the nurse walked past my bed on her way back to the nursing station, I apologized for asking her to rush right over for nothing. She smiled and gave me the "don't sweat it" sign with her hand.

The rest of the day was uneventful, and I was happy to go home.

November 22

Back at my house, my spine started to feel better. I've been wearing pocket-less pyjamas most days, so I needed a way to carry my wallet, keys, nail polish, etc. I decided to try and find a fanny-pack (AKA hip-sack), but I think stores stopped selling them after around 1989. So, naturally, I turned to Facebook for help:

Does anyone in or near Hamilton have a fanny-pack they'd like to sell? Any colour will do, as long as it's black – because I need to look cool when I wear it.

The first reply came from a lady named Carolyna Lovely:

Carolyna: "Oh good Christ! Just because you're dying doesn't mean you can digress to the worst fashion faux pas in history! Check these out, doll..." (She then gave me a link to some "modern man bags.")

Me: "Carolyna, you win the contest for the best FB comment ever. That made my day. But don't waste your time worrying about my fashion sense. That left the station a long time ago. That's why I have my shirt off in so many of my Facebook posts."

Carolyna: "Shirtless never goes out of style when one looks like you, darlin'!"

Anyway, a cool black leather fanny pack was dropped off at my house the next day. Isabel still doesn't grow tired of making fun of me when I wear it.

November 26

Isabel's brother, Mathias, is a great guy. He knew I needed to get out of the house, so he invited me over to his place to watch the Grey Cup game with the boys. I was glad to go, to hang out with them. I don't actually know how to watch a football game. I sometimes attend a game for the camaraderie (as well as the beer and chicken wings), but I don't understand the game, and I'm too embarrassed to ask the guys what the hell's going on. I just cheer when everyone else does. Shoot, I hope Mathias doesn't read this.

Dec 8

This is my advance apology for the rant that is to follow. I'm having a rough couple of days. I've got some potentially bad news to be received on Tuesday, with respect to the number of tumours inside me. In the meantime, I have anorexia again—you know the feeling you get after an all-you-can-eat buffet, when you and your stomach are regretting that third plate? I feel that way all the time now—all food disgusts me. I'm losing tons of weight. But I still have my beautiful wife and kids, my sister, brother, mother, my great music school, and my killer rock band (and people on Facebook who put up with my rants). PLUS, *Star Wars Episode 8* comes out this week, so it's hard to complain TOO much.

December 12

Today was the first day starting my new cancer treatment. It's immunotherapy with one of two different drugs added. I'd mentioned previously that one version killed a couple of people, whereas the other version had cured some folks. Luckily, the computer chose the good one for me. I was excited to get started.

As is always the case with clinical trials, the nurse has to disclose the side-effects that had occurred in patients during the earlier phases. This time, I was given the choice to read them or not. I chose not. I didn't want my subconscious brain to start anticipating new maladies.

Dr. Kapoor asked if I was able to give another guest appearance at one of his lectures. As always, I readily agreed. As before, I sat at the front of a lecture hall, facing the audience. But this time, there was a screen above and behind me, on which a live video of a nephrectomy was being projected. Nephrectomy is the fancy word for "kidney removal".

After about thirty minutes, my speech was interrupted. Apparently, the surgery was complete, and one of the surgical assistants was on her way to bring in the newly-removed kidney, complete with an attached tumour. All the students in the audience gathered around, and Dr. K asked me if I wanted to hold it. Darn tootin', I did. I put on some gloves and held out both my hands. The kidney was heavier than I'd thought it would be, and I could see the tumour that had taken it over. A girl next to me asked if I wanted my photo taken while holding the offending organ. "Absolutely," I replied. As my hands were quite occupied, I shifted my waist so the girl could remove my phone from my back pocket. She took a photo, and I thought for a moment that it would be a gas if I were to upload the image onto Facebook. But I knew that more than a few people would lose their minds. I also elected to not include the photo in this book, for the same reason. You're welcome.

Well, shit. I have another tumour in my spine now, and they suspect the cancer may also have spread to my brain—these are in addition to the tumours in my lungs, near my heart, and in my vertebrae. I take comfort in the fact that my brain works well (so far—read on). I try to go to bed a little less stupid every day. But lately it's been the opposite. A couple nights ago at home, I answered a call from a telemarketer who inquired if I'd like to do a survey.

I thought it over. Isabel looked at me strangely, as she was still surprised that I'd had the strength to even answer the phone. "Absolutely," I replied, to the girl at the other end of the line. "Let's do this."

"Wonderful," she said. "May I start by asking you your age?"

I thought it over, and then replied definitively that I was 25. Isabel, beside me on the couch, corrected me. "What? You're not 25, you're 46."

I grimaced. "Are you sure? I'm pretty sure I'm 25."

"You're not."

The girl on the phone just figured that I was messing with her, so she hung up. I was disappointed, as I'd been looking forward to taking her survey.

It was soon bedtime, so I scooped up the TV remotes and put them in my pocket—even though our sole TV is in the living room. Isabel asked me what the heck I was doing with the remotes, but I had no reply to give her. She then asked me some skill-testing questions, and I answered them well enough that I didn't have to check into Emergency.

A phone call to the doctor the next day meant that I had to go in for an MRI, to see if I had a brain tumour. In the end, it came back negative. We were very relieved.

December 17

How to be a good friend to someone with cancer (as compiled by my friends with cancer):

- Offer to visit me; don't wait for me to ask you. But please don't show up unannounced. Make it easy for me to say no. If I've said no twice, stop asking. That doesn't mean I don't want to see you, it just means I don't have the energy for guests right then.

- During a visit, if I fall asleep mid-sentence, don't feel badly. It's not you, it's me.

December 26

My daughter Meghan and I went out to do some Boxing Day shopping. Isabel was uneasy with me driving and she suggested that she come with me, to drive. But I didn't want to be a burden. I was feeling good that day; I was not mentally impaired, and I'd had no extra meds. Plus, Isabel had no interest in Boxing Day shopping, so I declined her kind offer of help. Meghan and I met up with my brother, Chris, and we hung out for a while and bought a few things. Afterward, Chris offered to drive me home, noting that I looked unwell. Again, I declined the help. Coming home, Meghan and I passed through Clappison's Corners, a very busy intersection just north of the city of Hamilton. A few seconds through the intersection, I passed out at the wheel. Thankfully, my car did not veer left towards oncoming traffic. Instead, it veered to the right, running off the road into a ditch— and then out of that ditch with a bang, as it ran into a copse of small trees. All four airbags deployed. My daughter was unscathed, though understandably shocked. We were stuck in the car, as the trees blocked our doors. A witness called 911, and the police showed up on the scene, along with an ambulance. But my daughter and I were both okay. My car ended up being a write-off.

January 2

I had asked again for an overnight helper, stated again that I preferred to have a guy over. Rachel Bolton contacted me. We've been friends since we were children. She addressed my concerns thusly:

"I know you said you don't want women to sleep over, but I want you to know that your silly reasons do not apply to me. You don't care if I see you cry. We've known each other since we were six, and I've seen you cry a bunch of times. Once more won't make a difference. You want somebody strong, in case you need someone to lift you up. Well, you know that I am one of the strongest people around. I've beaten you in wrestling and arm wrestling. And that was before cancer. Lastly: I'm a threat to nobody's marriage. You know it and I know it."

So, Rachel came over to my house that evening, and spent the night. I needed her to do a few things that were potentially embarrassing, and it was great. She was great. And my marriage was unscathed.

January 5

Anorexia is a weird thing. My kitchen, my fridge, are full of delicious, nutritious food. But nothing appeals to me. I just don't want to eat. They say to listen to your body, but my body says

I'm full and I don't need any food. So I have to eat against my will. It's not much fun.

January 8

I've realized it's irresponsible of me to inform Facebook-Land that I have a cancer that's potentially terminal, and then go silent for a while, leading people to wonder what the heck is going on. The fact is that, I try hard to post only the good stuff, and when there's nothing good to share, I tend to stay silent, rather than complain online all the time. The fact is that I am dropping weight like it's going out of style, and I am having a very hard time with things. But I still have my family, and my guitar. Life is actually good, despite the fact that, these days, I seem to be in pain all day long. It's quite a nuisance. Cancer really does suck.

January 10

I am in a very dark place, and no amount of positivity from friends will help. Lately, the pain I endure is so great that I call out wishing I could just die, as it appears only death would provide me with the respite I so crave. My Facebook posts of late have been a bit of a ruse, in that I show myself to be significantly stronger than I really am. Lately, I am prone to bouts of crying, though I try to hide them from my wife. Currently, I am dependent on Isabel to wait on me all day and night. And when she goes to work, I am dependent on friends and family to look after me. But it's mostly Isabel who takes the brunt of things. She works at the hospital as a nurse, then comes home and nurses me. I am scared that this is my new normal now. I've got shows booked with my band, and I don't know how the heck I'm going to get through them. But I get joy from my wife, my kids, my family and friends, though I fear I'll bring them down. Sometimes my kids witness my pain, and it tears me apart. So I turn to Facebook, as I enjoy reading, posting and commenting on the trials of others. It helps me a great deal to read and address the opinions in matters on social justice. This is where I'm at right now.

Jan 11

Twice I heard the clunk-sound of my wedding ring slipping off my finger. I have lost over sixty pounds since cancer struck me. I am skinny in a very unhealthy way, and my wedding ring won't stay on. I made a vow when I first put it on, so now I wear it around my neck.

January 12

Since passing out at the wheel last month, I voluntarily gave up driving, at least until my meds could be sorted out. This meant that Isabel did the driving, unless she was at work. In this case, I had to reply on friends to haul my kids and me around.

This afternoon, my very kind friend Julia offered to drive me to pick up the kids from school. I was in a bit of pain, but I had to accompany her, because my kids had not yet met Julia, and they would be apprehensive about getting into her car. There was a helluva snow storm, and it took us much longer than usual to get to the school. On the way home I had a spasm in my leg. It hurt like the devil, and I howled in pain throughout the journey. Poor Julia; she and my poor kids had to listen to this. Over the next few days, the spasms became worse.

January 14

Fran is someone I know only through Facebook. She kindly offered to bring a meal to me at my house. I accepted happily, and explained that I wouldn't be able to do much of a visit, as I was very weak of late. That afternoon, a car pulled into my driveway. Fran emerged, carrying a bag of food, and the car pulled away. Once in my living room, she plunked herself down on my couch and talked at me until I could take it no more. I asked her to leave, but she said she could not, as her ride would not be back for an hour or so. Then I became angry at Fran's presumption that I could entertain her for all this time. But anger takes a great deal of energy, and so I was thoroughly drained. I just fell asleep, while she sat there waiting for her ride to return.

January 15

Michelle Slote has been my friend since we were children. She is a hairdresser, and she does a great job on me, trying her best to make me look like Tom Cruise.

For some reason, I'd decided I needed my haircut, as I was looking rather crazy, of late. I knew there was no way I'd be able to make it to Michelle's salon, so I boldly asked her if she could come to my house to cut my hair. Being the kind person that she is, she came over the next afternoon with her scissors and such.

Poor Michelle. When she arrived at my place, I was in agony. I asked if she could cut my hair while I lay on the couch. But she explained that I needed to sit up. I told her I can only sit up for about a minute at a time. So Isabel propped me up on the couch while Michelle chopped away at my locks, as quickly as she could. After a minute, I said I needed to lie down. So she gave me some time to recuperate, then she continued when I could sit up again. I lasted another sixty seconds, and then told her I was done. I lay back down on the couch and cried in agony. With such care, Michelle continued to cut my hair as best she could. After Michelle left, Isabel brought me a mirror, and I saw that I did indeed look like Tom Cruise.

January 17

My damn leg spasms had become intolerable, such that we decided to drive to the Emergency department. I had an MRI for my spine booked for two days hence, but we couldn't wait. Also, my right leg was not working properly anymore.

On the way out to the car, I fell on the icy, snow-covered walkway. I couldn't move, and I was hurting pretty badly. So Isabel called an ambulance, and I got driven to the hospital once again. Thankfully, I was admitted right away. They did a scan, and saw that I needed surgery. I don't remember much, except that I was in a bed on a ward somewhere, waiting to be brought in.

The leg spasms had been brought on by the injury to my spine. They seemed to come every twenty to sixty minutes or so. Isabel gently massaged my leg to make the spasms subside. It was hellish.

After several hours of waiting, my dear mother arrived to give Isabel a break. My wife went home to try and get some sleep, while my mum waited beside me, spending the night in a chair at the foot of my bed.

In the morning, Isabel returned and took over. She took over in the chair, and didn't leave my side. We waited for two more days until it became my turn. Occasionally, she slept on the hospital floor.

I had been fasting the entire time. There was a notice by my bed that stated, "NPO" (Latin for "Nothing By Mouth"). It had been explained to me that they would cancel my surgery if I so much as licked a jujube. But I wasn't hungry anyway.

The doctors and nurses did not know how to deal with my pain. I had been on a pain pump at home, but it was not a sanctioned method of combating pain in the spinal unit. They had no protocol for the nurses to follow. Isabel had brought my pain pump along, and we used it, but the staff was not allowed to help. The problem was that they didn't know how to convert the amount of medicine I was getting from the pump to give me the right dose via IV. We were told they were conferring about it, and were going to call Dr. Slaven, the pain specialist looking after me, for advice, but they never did. Just before I had gone into surgery, they took out the pain pump. Thankfully, they gave me pain meds in my IV after that, and it all worked out.

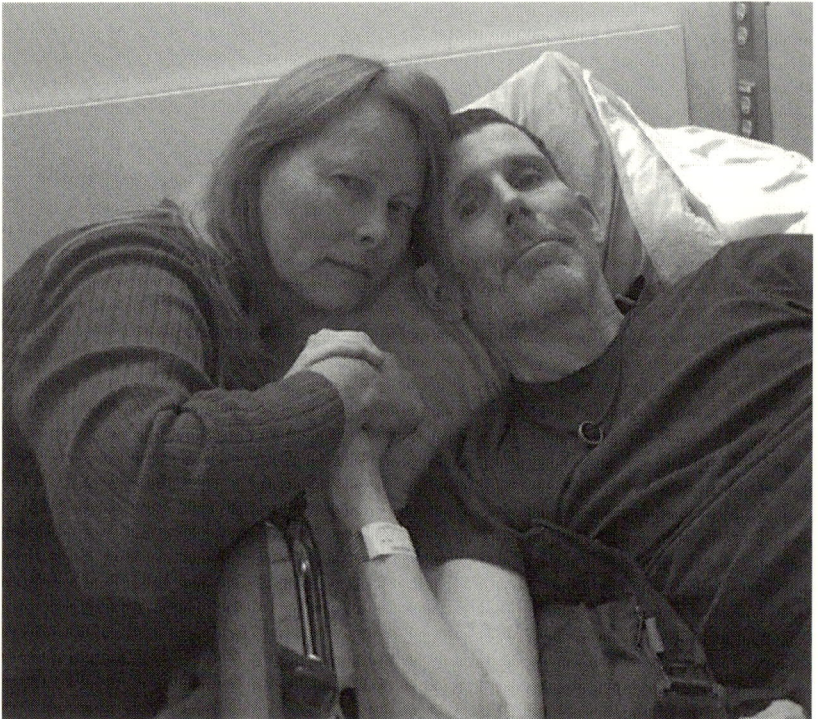

January 20

At ten PM, after waiting for three days, I was wheeled into the operating room. I was quite out of sorts. This surgery was a big deal (not like the Kyphoplasty). One of my vertebrae had completely shattered. I needed rods and screws in my back to hold me together – and they gave me a ten-inch-long scar on my back to prove it.

Like many people, I have a habit of becoming a fool in the time following anaesthesia. This day was no different. The first afternoon in recovery, I noticed a tube being fed right into my arm. It was apparently for my pain meds. I said aloud to nobody in particular: "I won't be needing this"—and I yanked it out of my arm. A young nurse walked by, and I called her over. I held out the end of the tube, and said, helpfully, "Here you go." I was actually quite proud of myself, and I gave her my most winning smile.

Looking at the bleeding area of my arm where the tube once was, the girl became upset. Actually, she was pissed right off. She yelled at me until I cried. None of the nurses on the floor were qualified to re-insert the tube into my arm, and that made her angrier. So they had to call a nurse from another unit to come do it. Trying to defuse the situation, I told her my wife could reinsert the tube, and I offered to call her up. The only problem was that I couldn't remember my wife's name.

Soon, another nurse arrived to save the day. She told me straight up that she was scared of what she had to do, as she'd only done that procedure a couple of times in the past. Usually, medical people work with such confidence that the patient becomes reassured. But this nurse was scared, and then so was I. It took a couple of attempts, but she finally inserted the tube back into my arm. Sometime later, I was transported into a step-down unit, a room I would occupy for the next several days.

Shortly after my supper, a new nurse came along to my bedside. She was one of the older nurses in the unit, and she had a kind, motherly face. She had to ask me some skill-testing questions, to make sure I was lucid. And I failed them all.

"Steve, what year is this?"

I thought about it carefully. I know I was born in 1971, and that I started school in 1976. I did some clever calculations, and then I looked her right in the eye. "It's 1997."

She made a note on her clipboard.

"Am I right?" I asked. I was hoping for a prize, to celebrate the ingenuity with which I figured out the current year.

The nurse smiled empathetically. "I'm afraid not. It's actually 2017."

"Oh, well I wasn't THAT far off – wait: *2017*? How long have I been out? Am I like that fairy tale guy who fell asleep for a bunch of years?"

The nurse chuckled softly. "You mean Rip Van Winkle? No, you're not."

"No," I started. "Wasn't Rip Van Winkle the German Shepherd in the black and white movies?"

"Nope. That was Rin Tin Tin."

I was getting more and more confused, and it was worrying me. But I wanted to continue until I could get something right. "I've got a great idea. How about if you ask me some *Star Wars* trivia, like: What's the name of Han Solo's ship? Why, that's easy. It's called—" I drew a complete blank. "Damnit. I forget."

She placed her hand on my shoulder and said, "Han's ship was the Millennium Falcon, sweetie."

I felt dejected. I used to be the king of *Star Wars* trivia. Looking back, it was actually pretty cool that the nurse knew the name of Han's ship.

Later that night, around midnight, I was awoken by the wailing of an old lady, not far from me. She was lamenting the fact the she was in a hospital. Without interruption, she cried, screamed and taunted the nurses. I knew it was going to be a long night. Nothing the nurses said or did could calm this lady down. Eventually, one of the male nurses lost his cool. He snapped at the lady, yelling, "Alice! We've had enough! You need to stop this!" Then Alice cried, and came up with a new thing to scream about: "I hate him!" It took over an hour for her to fall asleep.

January 21

Pain is so relative. In a hospital ward, we often get asked, "On a scale of 1 to 10, what's your pain?" Ten means you'd rather be dead. The old lady in the bed next to mine was moaning in pain, dying for relief. The nurse rushed in and asked a few questions, among them was, "On a scale of 1 to 10, what's your pain?"

The lady said, "It's 15!" The nurse made a note on her pad, replied that she would get some pills very soon, and then exited. Immediately after, the old lady called out to me, "Hey, do you have a phone charger I can borrow?" Every day is a lesson. Nobody with a pain level of 15 out of 10 can talk about anything but the sweet release of death. I've had a few Level 9s but they were brief. At home, my crazy leg spasms were an 8, but they lasted 20 minutes each time, making them unbearable.

January 23

I started to regain a bit of strength, but I was extremely weakened from my surgery, three days of no food, my cancer and pain meds, etc. It took me a while to realize I was paralyzed from the waist down. This was the result of the tumour on my spine, and the ensuing surgery. I started to get worried about being in a wheelchair for the rest of my life. When I needed to turn myself in bed, I needed two nurses to do it for me. I couldn't even help them; I was useless. My pain was mostly under control, except for when they had to move me. I was partly in control of my pain meds, in that I could give myself extra doses of morphine with my IV. But I kept forgetting to use it, as my head wasn't clear. Isabel had to continually remind me to push the button.

Here in Canada, we often watch the news in the US with incredulity. Most of us here thought it was disgusting the way Donald Trump banned people from Muslim countries from entering The States. It didn't matter if they were US citizens visiting the Middle East and trying to return home to America. He ruined many lives with that proclamation. I thought about this when speaking to the surgeon who fixed my spine. Dr. Saleh Almenawer is regarded as a genius in the field of spinal surgery. He is from the Middle East. In fact, his resident doctors and assistants were also Arabic. And, without exception, they were kind, knowledgeable and incredibly skilled. I'm sure they feel lucky to be in Canada, rather than the US – and Canada is certainly lucky to have them.

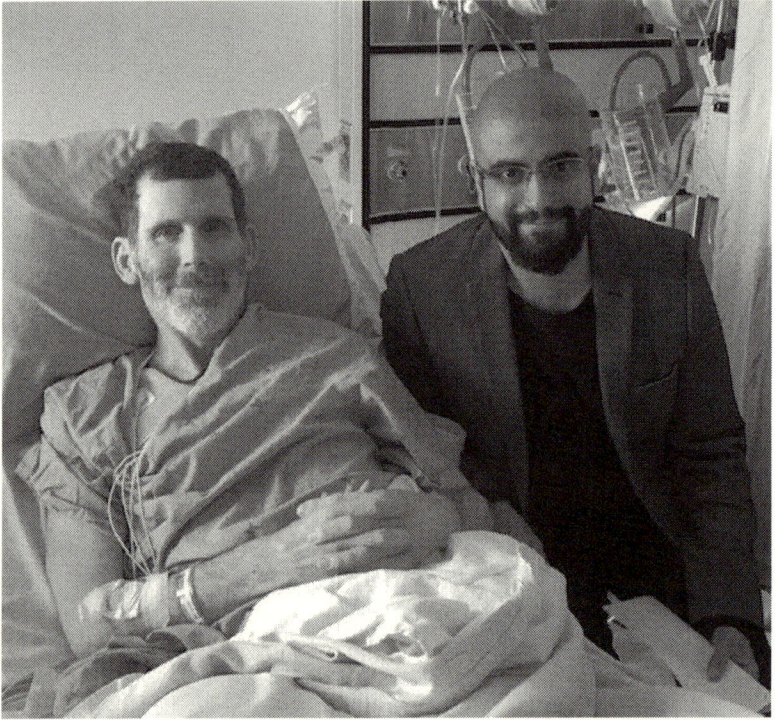

January 24

Dr. Almenawer was wonderful to me. During the surgery, he'd inserted a rod and pins to my spine. He often stopped by to check on my recovery and my progress. He told me that my spinal column was intact, and no damage had happened to it. He saw that, while my left leg had a bit of mobility, my right leg was useless. The doctor looked me right in the eye and promised me that I would walk again. I believed him, but it was certainly frustrating not to be able to move.

January 25

Virginia's bed was directly across from mine. She was 85 years old, and was recovering from knee surgery. She was lucid and kind. She also had an enormous family. They kept coming and coming, contrary to the rules about visitors. Just when I thought I wouldn't be able to take any more of the constant party, I realized that Virginia felt the same way. So in the middle of day two, whenever her gang came in after that, she would just go to sleep. The nurses picked up on what was going on, and they started to intervene.

Virginia's husband, Ed, was a kind and gentle man. He came to visit her every day. He was usually there at the same time as Isabel, so the four of us often chatted. One day, after Isabel had arrived, Virginia said to Ed, "Look at the young couple there," and she pointed to Isabel and me. "Every time she arrives, she gives him a kiss. And every time she leaves, she gives him another kiss. Eddie, I want you to do that to me. When you get here, give me a hello kiss, and when you leave, give me a goodbye kiss."

Poor Ed turned around and gave me a look that said, "Gee whiz, lad, thanks a LOT." The funny thing is that they've been married for 50 or 60 years, and I was thinking about what I could learn from them, about the longevity of a marriage. I didn't think my wife and I could teach them anything.

The guy in the hospital bed right next to me was around my age, and was trying very hard to die. He'd been giving the nurses a hard time about everything. After the nurses stepped out, I had a chat with the guy about being nicer to them.

"But why do I have to have that stupid tube up my nose?"

"It helps you breathe," I told him.

After a pause, he replied with conviction, "I don't want to breathe anymore." Later on, the nurses were unable to revive the man from sleep, and his vitals started to slip. They brought in the crash cart, and the team rushed into action. It was very disconcerting for me, being so close to someone who could quite possibly die in front of me. After a few minutes, they hauled the poor guy down to ICU. I tried to send him good vibes, hoping he'd pull through.

January 27

Lying in the hospital bed, being unable to move, was not at all fun. The nurses had to come in and turn me over every four hours or so. On this night, I buzzed for the nurse, asking her to help me turn over, as I was in a great deal of discomfort. She replied that it wasn't time yet, and that she'd be by in about an hour. The discomfort then turned to pain. It was around 11pm at night, so I couldn't call anyone to come to the hospital and help me. Instead, I trolled Facebook for help—again. A woman around my age, name of Janice, replied, and said she'd be right over. We'd never met each other, never even crossed paths on FB, but she came over anyway, only because I'd asked for help.

This gives you an idea about the kind of person Janice is. When she arrived at my room, the first thing she did was turn me over—her mother was an occupational therapist, so she knew a bit about what to do. When I was settled, Janice brought out snacks. Then she produced a book, an autobiography by the singer, Patty Smith. I had insomnia, so the book was nice to have. Janice stayed all night in a chair by my bed, reading out loud until I fell asleep sometime in the wee hours of the morning. What a kind person she is.

Later, when I contacted Janice to thank her, she explained what had gone on before coming to the hospital. It had been a little bit of a rough night for her, and she asked, "Lord, make me an instrument of Your peace." Before going to bed, she checked on Facebook once more and saw my post, asking for help. Her request had been answered, and she decided to go out and lend a hand to someone who needed it, keep him company. Enough people have been so good to her in her life, it was time to share.

January 28

I had not been able to do any physiotherapy since the surgery, except for wiggling my toes on one foot. The therapists needed me to be able to sit up in my chair for two hours straight before they would start. I had to get hauled out of my bed with a hoist and plopped into a chair. At first, I could only sit up for fifteen minutes before I'd had enough. Very slowly, over a number of days, I increased the amount of time I could sit up.

January 29

I turned over in my bed by myself for the first time tonight. This was no small feat. But then I forgot the cables on the other side of the bed (one for my pain meds injection, one to call a nurse, and my iPhone power cable) and everything became tangled. Also, I'd had a hard time eating. But I was hungry tonight, which is something to be celebrated. So at 3:30 AM, Bob Foster, a guy I knew from high school, showed up at the hospital with a large bowl of spaghetti. It was delicious. And he moved my cables over for me.

Then there was George, my new roommate. He arrived an hour ago, and his heart started acting up, which had the nurses all running around, and doing things other than refilling my cup of water. Again, it's a good thing I had Bob there.

January 30

One of the joys of having a music school is in watching the students grow up, move on, and pursue careers in music. Often, I receive CDs from former students, and I love hearing what they are doing. Rob Brown studied guitar with us for years. I watched him develop a band and record his songs and I encouraged him from afar. This afternoon, Rob emailed me with a link to his newest song, asking if I could give it a listen. The only problem was that the silly little speakers on my phone wouldn't do the song any justice, and I needed to listen with some volume. The answer was for me to wait until my room was to be cleaned up, because I knew the pretty girl with the mop always had her ear bud headphones on while she worked.

"Hi Rachel," I greeted her when she arrived a little later. "Say, is there any chance I could borrow your ear buds for four minutes? There's a song I need to listen to."

Rachel happily popped the buds out of her ears, and handed them over. "I'll pass back here in a while," she said.

I sat back and listened to Rob's new song. It was called "You and Me", by his band, The Ruddy Ruckus. I fell in love with it. When Rachel returned to my room, I motioned her over. I wiped her ear buds clean and gave them back, but kept the jack plugged into my phone. "Here," I said. "Give this song a listen."

By the way Rachel bounced up and down, I knew she also loved the song. After she left, I thought about this band, and what I could do to make them famous. At that moment, stuck in a hospital ward, I knew I couldn't do much more than to share their song online. Afterward, I turned to the other part of my day, thinking about what flavour pudding they would bring me. My career as a band manager would have to wait.

February 3

AJ is one of my guitar students. He's a good kid, and a talented player. I'd had to put his lessons on hold (along with those of my other students) while I was in the hospital. AJ's parents sent me a text, asking if their boy could visit me here. I said that would be fine, but I suggested he bring his guitar—and his music stand

and book. This way we could do a full guitar lesson. It worked out really well, as AJ showed up many times during the course of my stay, guitar in tow.

February 4

My sister, Jenny, visited me, with her husband and their two wonderful teenage girls. We had a great visit, and then the nurse came in and told me that I was to move to another room. The room I had been in since the surgery was a step-down room people go to when they need lots of nursing help. I wanted to pull out a calendar and ask the nurse when a good day would be (perhaps on the 17th?). The nurse smiled and told me I would be moving right that moment. Isabel had pre-packed some of my belongings a few days earlier, in anticipation of this very event. But I still had possessions all over the place, including drawings on the wall from my kids and my nieces.

Jenny's family packed everything and followed as my bed was wheeled to the room next door. There was only one other bed there, so I was happy. Then I met my roommate. Holy smokes. Ron was there because they had to remove one of his legs—he apparently did not look after his diabetes. He also didn't look after his teeth, or his belly. And he was loud when he spoke. Boy, was he loud. When Ron's sister was visiting, they screamed at each other for a while. Then, after she went home, he called her and they argued again, at full volume.

Through the curtain that sometimes divided our beds, Ron inserted himself into all my conversations, with each of my visitors, no matter the topic. He would chime in with such gems as, "That's the guv-ment's fault. Ya wanna know why...?" or, "'Cause all them doctors are just stupit."

My friend, Dr. Karen Raymer, is an anaesthesiologist at this hospital. One evening after her shift, she stopped by my room for a visit, with the idea that she and I would have a nice long talk. I was very happy to see her. Almost immediately, Ron threw his verbal diatribes at us, and Karen and I weren't able to converse. Karen gave me a look, then said, "J'ai une bonne idée. On va continuer comme ça." I glanced over at Ron, and he didn't budge, didn't say a word. It was perfect. Karen and I continued our talk in French, and Ron was silent.

February 5

I was trying to figure out why all the nurses were ignoring me, each time I tried to call somebody with my little intercom button. I would buzz, someone would answer, then hang up as I tried to speak. Eventually, I learned that the microphone on my end didn't work well. When I buzzed the nursing station, I could get out about two syllables before the connection was lost. Whenever my bed number showed up at the nursing station's intercom system, I'm sure the poor nurses rolled their eyes at my apparent rudeness. I was unable to say, "I'm sorry to bother you, but when you have a spare moment, would you mind bringing me a new pee bottle? Thanks so much." Instead, I had to yell out, "Pee bottle!"

There was irony in the fact that Ron's intercom worked just fine. And he was as curt as I appeared to be: He would shout things like, "Get me some water."

February 6

Ron was blessedly discharged. He left unceremoniously, and two cleaning ladies descended upon our room to clean and disinfect his area. Ron had been there for three months. One of the ladies asked if I wanted to transfer to Ron's side of the room, as it was near the window. Even though I relished the idea of a working intercom, I had to decline, because I was certain the nurses had long been associating Ron's bed number with his belligerence.

February 7

I was soon able to leave my bed and get into a wheelchair. The physiotherapist used a slider board on which I slid my butt from the bed to the chair. Eventually, I was brought to a fancy machine that hauled me up onto my feet, supporting me all the way. The next part was to be able to take a few steps, aided by this device. It was very hard work.

My new roommate was a quiet lady named Jan, who had recently emerged from surgery on her arm. At around midnight, Jan was awake and was aware of her surroundings, though only partially. She had a crazy device that was hooked up to her. I think it was her IV. Every time she bent her arm, an alarm would go off, a loud, incessant beep that insured nobody in that part of the unit could sleep. Each time she bent her arm, it triggered the crazy alarm. The nurse's solution was to tell her not to bend her arm. That worked for 60 seconds, after which point she bent her arm, and the alarm rang out once again. I begged the nurses to silence the alarm once and for all. It took 20 minutes of them going back-and-forth to readjust things, and they finally disabled it.

Then Jan told me she needed to leave her bed to go to the washroom. I tried to explain to her that she probably had a catheter and a diaper, and that she was good to go with what she had. But she didn't understand, and she moaned for much of the night.

"I have to pull this out," I heard her say. Good god, no. I didn't know which tube she was talking about, but it didn't matter. Pulling anything out would result in me not getting sleep again. Trying to insert empathy into my voice, I shouted over to her to NOT pull anything out. Thankfully, she heeded my words. It was a very rough night.

February 8
My friend Tomas posted on Facebook that he had lost another amigo to cancer, and that he was sad. He gave no other details, and didn't give the name of the deceased. One of the comments

beneath his post read, "Was that Steve? That's too bad, he was a nice guy."

I quickly posted a reply. "Nope. I'm still here." But the idea really hit home.

The person about whom Tomas had written turned out to be Daniel, the husband of my friend Rick. Daniel was a very nice man. He and Rick were so happy together. I will miss him.

Isabel arrived at the side of my hospital bed with three bottles of pills she'd brought from home: Oxycocets for pain, Hydromorphone for pain, and Zopoclone (sleeping pills). The reason I needed my own stash of pills was that it often took an hour for the nurses to respond and administer the drugs (they had the same drugs for me on hand). It takes another 45 minutes for the pills to kick in. I wanted to keep my own supply so I didn't have to be a bother to the nurses. As for the sleeping pills, the nurses gave me a hard time for each one, as the doctor only gave permission for one pill at a time. For each instance, we had to call for permission, and go through the process all over again. Isabel knows me, and knows that I don't abuse my meds. In fact, she often had to encourage me to use them.

I stashed the three pill bottles in the drawer of my bedside table, the one that extends over my bed so I can eat. A porter was in the room at the time, and she saw the contraband pills. She told me I was not allowed to have my own meds, and then she ran out of the room at full speed to tattletale at the nursing station. Luckily for me, I knew that the nurse was not fluent in English, and that the porter's tattletale would die right then and there. The porter returned to my room and gave me a smug smile, happy that she was doing her duty, unaware of the fact that her message didn't make it through. And I kept my pills.

February 10

This was the day for The Great Hospital Wheelchair Races of 2018. My new friend, Bo, didn't speak much English, but he understood that he and I were to race our wheelchairs all the way down the hall of our unit. I talked one of the busy nurses into taking a moment to count off at our starting line. I actually won the first heat and moved on to the semi-finals. But I couldn't find anyone brave enough to race me again, now that I was a champion. The great Rick Hansen would be amused, I'm sure.

I'd posted the photo of Bo's and my race on Facebook, and someone actually doubted my claim of victory, to which I replied, "Truth be told, we went about point-five miles per hour, and often collided with each other. I'm not sure who actually won, but we giggled ourselves silly."

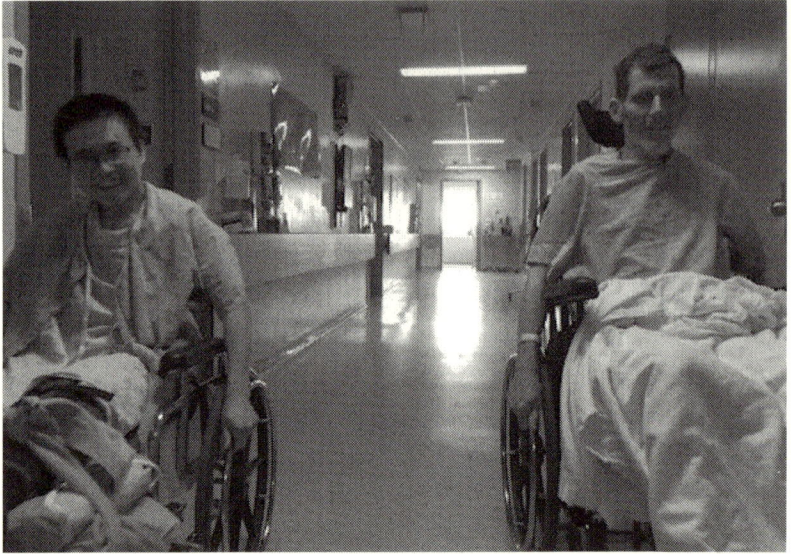

February 12

Wayne Krawchuk has been a dear friend to my family since the 1970's. When I was a child, I used to love watching him play guitar and sing in his band. He gave me my first guitar when I was ten.

Wayne came by the hospital this afternoon, and I was overjoyed to see that he had brought his guitar with him. My mum was there in the room, staying with me. I was happy to hear Wayne play us a couple of wonderful songs from his new album. Then I asked him if he knew the song "Helplessly Hoping" by Crosby, Stills & Nash. He smiled, and told me he certainly did. I reached out my hand, and he passed me his gorgeous Larivée guitar. I hadn't played in so long, and I wasn't even sure I'd be able to make any sounds. But I just hit the opening chords and finger-picked my way through the intro part. Without any discussion about who would sing which part, Wayne, my mum and I just started singing in three-part harmony. The hallway traffic came to a halt; a few of the nurses popped in to listen. It was a wonderful moment.

February 14, 3:30 AM

A Short Essay on Love, By Steve Parton

Poets from Shakespeare on down have tried to define love, to put it into tangible words. In 1961, Jubal Harshaw opined on it as being "The condition in which another person's happiness is essential to your own." If we are to accept this definition, to consider it as truth, then I love (and am loved by) a great many people.

I'm astounded at how often I end a missive or a face-to-face conversation with "I love you", "I love you too," or even "Love ya, man." I am surrounded by so much love that it overwhelms me at times when I consider it all.

Now, the feeling may at first blush seem like when a child numbers all his friends, say, for a birthday party. There was, naturally, a lack of depth and sincerity in that endeavour. High school and college found me with a small but loyal base of friends, relationships founded on the way we shared intimate thoughts and philosophies. And now I care about the spouses and children of my high school friends.

But what about my wife and children? They know they are not lumped in with everyone else, and that I love them most of all. My wife has received her own composition for this day of saints, written by me in the dark hours of the hospital night.

(In case you're wondering, my Jubal Harshaw reference is from *Stranger In A Strange Land*, by Robert A. Heinlein).

February 17

This past December, my family and I attended the opening night screening of *Star Wars Episode 8*. My kids loved it. Me, I passed out in the first few minutes, and missed the whole thing. So my brother Chris had an idea. I'd been here in the hospital for a month, and he decided it was time to break me out, to go see the *Star Wars* film (again). I actually asked for a day pass, and it was granted.

Chris helped me out of my bed, and into the wheelchair. The nurses gave us a wooden sliding board, with which I could transfer myself between the wheelchair and the passenger seat of Chris' car. This was my first time being out in public, and it felt great. The experience gave me real sympathy for people who are in a wheelchair permanently.

We went to a small theatre in nearby Burlington, as it was the only place still showing this film. The theatre claimed to be wheelchair accessible, but it was not. Basically, they had removed one chair from the audience area and put up a sign with the wheelchair symbol. But my chair wouldn't fit, so I sat in the aisle and blocked the entire row. And each time a child had to go pee, I had to move my chair. But it was still an adventure. I'm very thankful to my brother for setting this all up.

February 23

Now that I was a man-about-town, Chris suggested we go out to a restaurant. So I asked for another day pass, and away we went. Somehow, we came up with the idea that we didn't need the slider board to get into Chris' car. My brother manhandled me out of the wheelchair, into the front seat of his car. He did the same thing at the restaurant. The act was a testament to his strength, and my skinny little body.

Today was Moving Day! I was to be transferred from the Hamilton General Hospital to the Juravinski Hospital (not to be confused with the Juravinski Cancer Centre next door to it). There was an intense rehabilitation program waiting for me, and I was excited to go. The nurses in my unit were all sad to see me leave. After I received my walking papers, they all came by my bed to see me off.

I travelled via a Patient Transfer vehicle from the old hospital to the new. It was a very bumpy ride; all the way there, it felt as if we were going to topple over on to the side.

February 24

There were three to a room where I was, in my new place at the Juravinski Hospital. My two roommates were Jim and Vincenzo, and both were older than Moses. Jim was mobile, and liked to get up throughout the night and wander about. Several times, he woke me up in the wee hours of the morning, asking if I wanted to play checkers, or go down to the boardwalk and check out the lasses.

My other roommate, Vincenzo, had a big family. They were all wonderful people, and they were all Italian. They came in droves, and were emphatic in their love for their papa. The first time they showed up, I was in the middle of a guitar lesson, teaching young AJ. Then came the cacophony of, "Hi, Papa!"

So rather than ask them all to talk quietly, I sent AJ out on a task. "Go to the lounge, just past room 12 on the left. Count how many people are in there, and then come on back."

AJ was back in a flash. "There's only one person there." So he and I took ten minutes to get me set up in my wheelchair. In due time I had his guitar, music stand, footstool and sheet music on my lap, and AJ pushed my chair into the lounge. The room's sole occupant saw the guitar, and shut off the TV, hoping for a concert. He listened to a few scales, then left the room out of boredom. AJ had a great lesson.

February 26

The Mykytyshyn sisters, Donna and Linda, are wonderful friends of mine. They showed up to my room with hugs, stories, and a mini beer fridge that used to belong to their brother Walter. The fridge was great; it had a beer logo on the front, and was just large enough to hold a six-pack. Linda plugged it in and put it on my bedside table. To boot, the two of them had stocked it, not with beer, but with juice, yogurt and pudding. It became a conversation piece to each doctor or nurse who arrived. When I was asked why I had beer in my room, I replied that it was to entertain guests, in case a party broke out.

February 27

My weight before cancer was 220 lbs. For the first couple of years I held steady around 180. When I checked into the hospital (via ambulance) I was 162. Today I clocked in at 143. Dr. Z gave me a lecture, telling me not to listen to my body while eating. If I didn't feel like eating, I had to eat it anyway. If I thought I might throw it up, I had to take a chance and eat anyway. I'd been following her advice, and I had yet to vomit. Also, Dr. Z told me that if I didn't eat more, they were going to fit me with a feeding tube. I didn't exactly know what that was, but it sure didn't sound like fun. So, I tried to teach myself how to love the food I was given each day.

February 28

Around mid-morning, I was visited by a pair of kind seniors possessing smiles and Bibles, a man and a woman. They announced they were from the hospital's church parish. They asked if I would like to receive communion, and for them to pray for me. I said both would be great, except that I'm not Catholic. The lady looked down at a clipboard and said, "My mistake." They abruptly showed me their backs as they turned to leave, and I felt rejected.

"Wait a minute," I said. "We both worship the same Saviour. You don't think we can find some common ground here?" Then I realized I was putting too much pressure on the old people. We weren't going to solve any centuries-old Catholic-Protestant issues this afternoon. In the end, she offered to recite the Lord's Prayer, which I accepted, if only to make her feel a bit less uncomfortable.

March 2

Isabel and I had a good visit, but it was time for her to leave. On her way out, she said, "By the way, Keith told me he was going to drop by to see you."

I started to panic. "What? Can you tell him I've been transferred to another hospital, maybe in Siberia?"

"Oh, it'll be fine. I'm sure he won't stay long. He said he's bringing a gift."

Shit. That makes things even worse. Not Keith.

Soon after Isabel left, the door to my room opened, and I braced myself. But it was only the doctor, there to discuss my meds. A few seconds after the conversation began, Keith arrived, bearing a big smile and a small plant. "Steeeeeveeee!"

I immediately started to feel guilty. I've known Keith for years. He's a nice guy, but he has the propensity to suck all my energy away, leaving me exhausted. "Hi Keith," I said. "Look, I'm busy talking with the doctor."

Every other human being I know understands that discussions with doctors get priority over just about everything. But not Keith. He turned to the doctor. "How long are you going to be? Stevie and I have some catching up to do!"

I replied for the doctor. "It doesn't matter, Keith. He will be as long as he wants to be. You need to wait."

But Keith was not to be swayed. He turned to the doctor. "Here's the thing: I have another friend to see at two o'clock, so I need to have my visit with Stevie right now." He gestured to the plant in his hands. "This plant is from Croatia, in South America."

His lack of geography almost distracted me. But I stayed focused. "Keith, you have to leave now. I'm trying to talk to the doctor."

But Keith barrelled on, as he had another gift. "And these chocolates are for you. There's a legend inside, because I know you don't like the ones with coffee."

"That's wonderful. Please leave now." I sent an apologetic look to the doctor.

"Okay, Stevie. I'll come back tomorrow, and we'll hang out for a while." As he took his leave, I started to think that I should actually transfer to a hospital in Siberia.

For the record, Keith is not the real name of the person in the anecdote above. But his words are written verbatim.

March 3

One of the reasons I'd been transferred to the Juravinski Hospital was because they had a very good rehabilitation program. Two or three times every day, I worked with the physiotherapists there. They had a device called an Alpha Walker. It's like a regular walker except the bars are elbow-height. With it, I could putter around the vast Rehab Room.

My friend, Pat Brooks, came by for a visit, and was kind enough to bring me my mandolin. It had been so long since I'd played, and I had melodies dancing around in my head. With the mandolin on my lap, I started composing a song. But I had no way of writing it down. So I asked Pat if I could dictate chords and notes to him, for him to write on his phone.

And he did. The whole thing reminded me (just a little bit) of the scene in the film *Amadeus* during which Mozart dictated his music to Salieri—only without the musical genius part. And I wasn't on my deathbed.

After the song was committed to Pat's phone, one of the nurses came into the room. She was French Canadian, so I sang her a song called "Jolie Louise", written by the beloved Hamilton musician Daniel Lanois.

When Pat left, I forgot all about the song I'd written. A few months later, he showed up at my house and showed me my song. I think it's a good one.

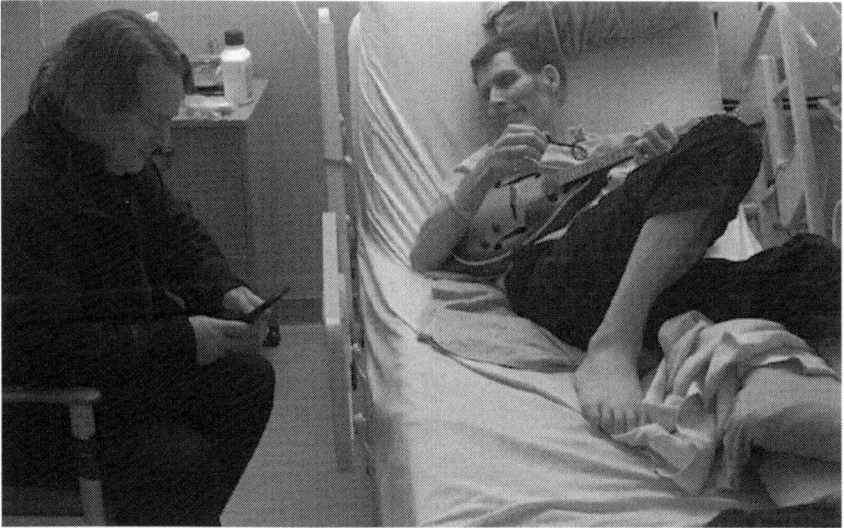

March 4

Eighty-two-year-old Marion was my new roommate for a few days. She occupied the bed next to mine. She had just had surgery, as she had fallen down a full flight of stairs, and was not recovering well. She was very high-maintenance. In my mind, I nicknamed her The Princess, as she treated everyone around her as if they were her royal subjects.

Last night, in the middle of the night, The Princess suddenly had enormous trouble breathing. I moved to call the nurse, and was prepared to shout out down the hall, but Marion had a fancy bed that told the nurse's station automatically when something was wrong. And indeed it was. Brittany was there in a flash. Up until then, I'd only seen Brittany administer meds, checks vitals, fluff pillows and fetch water.

Before long, there was a team of medical people around Marion's bed. My own bed was pushed aside to accommodate the circus next to me. Brittany, as Marion's principal nurse, was expected to recall every number she'd measured from this patient. She did just that. Brittany's performance was incredible as the two doctors held her to account for what she'd administered to The Princess. I was duly impressed.

March 5

The Princess was in full form today as we had a new nurse, a young girl named Nikki. Her Royal Highness decided she would no longer swallow pills, and that she required all meds to be crushed in apple sauce before she would take them. Poor Nikki left to do The Princess' bidding. When she returned with a little bowl of crushed meds, I said to her, "That's a great idea! I've just decided that I would also like my meds crushed in apple sauce. Or maybe raspberry yogurt."

Later that morning, the physiotherapist came in to start my day's stretching. I was to do the boring foot exercises in my bed before going out to the Rehab Room to do my boring rehab exercises. But Vincenzo's family was there with us. I think the population of Sicily was considerably reduced, judging by the number of people in our room. The physiotherapist became a little frustrated that I was unable to hear her over the racket, so she turned to leave, saying she'd be back in a minute.

When she returned, she announced that I was being moved to a solitary room. She helped me pack my things, then I was pushed in my bed down the hall to a room by myself. This new place was fantastic. It was a corner room, and I had windows on two walls. I was very happy.

March 10

I had a CAT scan the other day, and the results were not good. All the tumours had expanded and spread. Worse, they spread also to my liver, and were too numerous to count. So Dr. Hotte took me off the immunotherapy, as that treatment clearly wasn't helping me. He told me I would be put on a chemotherapy again, a new drug called Cabozantinib (Cabo). It was an experimental drug and, though it was being used in the US and in Britain, it had not yet been approved in Canada. Dr. Hotte applied for me to be able to receive the drug on a compassionate basis, as I had no other options left. He arranged for the pills to be shipped from the UK. Once again, Dr. Hotte demonstrated his dedication to his patients.

I was a bit apprehensive about this chemo. My friend Paul Scott, who also has kidney cancer, had to stop taking this same drug because it was giving him heart troubles. I didn't want to have heart troubles. The doc explained to me that Cabo would be very hard on my body. He also explained that if I didn't take this drug I wouldn't make it to May 2-4 Weekend. And that would stink, because I would miss the new *Star Wars* movie (*Solo*, coming out May 25).

But back to reality for a moment: this news was very hard on Isabel and me, as we started to worry about what was to come. This new chemo was not unlike the chemo I'd had a couple of years back. That one was called Sutent, and it made me feel weak all the time, but I'd had no choice back then – just like I had no choice but to agree to take Cabo now.

The thing is, these cancer meds are hit and miss. They can work on some people, but not for others. And the side-effects can be different for everyone. We didn't know if Cabo would work for me. There was a real possibility that I only had two more months left to live. We were scared.

March 17

I often transfer from my bed to my wheelchair, or my wheelchair to a vehicle, and I have become quite good at it. I can do it easily now, in almost any circumstance. I no longer need someone to spot me.

My nurse today was a petite Asian lady named Ling. She spotted me as I transferred from my bed to my wheelchair. Halfway through the procedure, my muscles gave out, and I fell forward. Immediately, Ling put her open palm on my chest and shoved me back. "You no fall on face today," she said, then went about her business.

March 22

I was to be discharged from the hospital in a few days. I had mixed feelings about that. I wanted so badly to go home, to be in my own bed, but I was still unable to walk unassisted. Even though I was making some strides with the Alpha Walker, it was all very frustrating.

March 28

After two and a half months in the hospital, I was now back home. I was very thankful for the support, visits and contraband meals I'd received. So now the next phase of my life was to begin, as I learned to cope with life in a wheelchair. With a good deal of help, Isabel had been retrofitting our house. We knew I wouldn't be able to make my way upstairs to our bedroom, so our bed was brought down to the family room, on the main floor. The problem was that I kept finding places I couldn't go, and things I couldn't do. It was an adjustment, to say the least. Also, I started on the new chemo, and the only side-effect that kicked in so far was fatigue. Give it time.

March 29

Over the past year or so, I've gotten to be good friends with Wayne Hodgson. We met over our mutual love of Triumph motorcycles, the difference being that he owns one, while I have a picture of one on my computer's opening screen. It's a Bonneville T100, if you care about that sort of thing. Before The Days of the Wheelchair, Wayne and I had been to a couple of concerts together. He knows a LOT of musicians and music industry folk.

Shortly after I returned home from my extended stay at the hospital, Wayne called me and invited me to a special performance in Toronto featuring the band The Rheostatics, with special guest Alex Lifeson on lead guitar. Alex is from the band Rush, and is my favourite guitarist on the planet. Wayne told me he'd made arrangements for me to attend the show with him, and then meet Alex backstage. I was beside myself with excitement, but then reality kicked in, and I knew I wouldn't be able to attend. It was all too much. I was sick as hell, and I was too weak to move. Add to this the fact that the concert was in a venue that was older than God, and not at all wheelchair accessible. And even worse was the fact that the Green room (change room) was probably on the second floor. It broke my heart, but I had to decline this once-in-a-lifetime invitation.

The next day, Wayne showed up at my house, kind man that he is. Standing in my doorway, he was hiding something large behind his back. He handed the large something over to me, and I saw that it was a guitar case. I opened it up to find a brand-new, white Les Paul electric guitar. On the face of it was largely scribed in marker: "To Steve. Happy strumming. Alex Lifeson". Wayne then showed me a few photos of Alex signing the guitar to me. The instrument is currently hanging on my living room wall, but I take it down often, to play Rush songs. What a good friend Wayne is.

April 12

Life was throwing me some more curveballs, but I took them on the chin. I was largely confined to a wheelchair, and I didn't know if I would ever walk freely again. I tried hard to get used to my new lot, but it was very frustrating. Isabel still did not complain, despite all the work she had to do. I had an incredible physiotherapist named Jean. She came to my house once a week, and had me do exercises to help me strengthen my legs, that I may one day walk again. The exercises were very boring, but I did them anyway.

We started renting an Alpha Walker. It was just like the one I'd used at the hospital, and it held me upright while I walked around the house. The hope was that, one day, I might be able to get around with a regular walker, or even a cane.

As the spring wore on, I became more and more weakened. I was not able to take the chemo everyday as I should have. The side effects increased, and became more intolerable. I could hardly eat, talk or swallow. It was a very rough time.

May 26

Lots of people got to see the movie *Solo* this weekend but, if you'll allow me to brag a little, I saw the film about three weeks ago, on May 6. We are only now able tell people what happened: A representative from Lucasfilm in California showed up at my house and let us watch the movie in a private advance-screening. Only four of us were permitted, so Nathan Fleet, one of my fellow devoted *Star Wars* fans; my brother; and my son were the lucky guys with me. My mother and sister had to stay home, consumed with jealousy. The Lucasfilm fellow inspected our living room: he disconnected the Wi-Fi and the telephone, so no illicit recordings could be made. It was spectacular, being able to see this in advance. And we all loved the movie. After it was over, the man packed up his laptop and promptly flew back to California.

Here's how this happened: The Juravinski Cancer Centre has an organization called Wellwood. They provide support services for cancer patients and their families. They're the ones who host my cancer support group. I don't know how, but Glen, one of the fellows who runs the group, had a conversation about me with one of the other volunteers there, who contacted Lucasfilm and explained that they had a diehard *Star Wars* fan in the cancer group, and could they make something happen. And they did. It'd been hard keeping it a secret all this time.

June 1

I was very ill, and was not myself, as evidenced by some of the stories herein. I spent almost all of everyday on the couch. I didn't read, watch TV or listen to music. I'd had a very rough time trying to run my music school, Avalon Music Academy. My mom, sister and niece, Katie, all took turns running the office. Finally, they held an intervention, and told me it was time to let the school go. This was very hard for me, as I'd had it for nineteen years. I'd franchised it out to several locations around Southern Ontario.

One of the franchisees is Krista. She owns the location in nearby Ancaster. Without wanting to appear as if she were taking advantage of someone's misfortune, Krista offered to buy me out a couple of years ago, not long after my diagnosis. Now, it was time. And it was actually a perfect fit. Krista knows exactly what she's doing, so there would be no training, no growing pains. I simply gave her the keys to the building. My brother Chris, the lawyer, came over to help me figure out the terms of the sale of my school. I remembered telling him to make sure the deal was fair for Krista, as she was not going to use a lawyer of her own.

Beyond that, I was mentally absent for the entire negotiation process. As my brother talked, I faded in and out of consciousness. I didn't even notice what the selling price was. Eventually I contacted Krista and asked her, "How much did I sell the music school to you for? I mean, how many millions?"

July 3

Last December I bought three tickets to go see Ian Anderson of Jethro Tull, who was to perform with his band in July, at the Budweiser Stage, an amphitheatre in Toronto that seats around 16,000 people. The plan was for me to attend with my friends Scott and Craig, the owners of Mountain Music Store (who are also big Jethro Tull fans). Craig's seat was in the 12th row, but Scott and I had tickets for the third row (!), right in the centre of the stadium, close enough to see Ian Anderson's sweat as he wails away on his flute. I bought the tickets before realizing I needed spinal surgery, before my weeks-long stay in the hospital, and before my wheelchair came along. As the July date approached, I began to worry that I would be unable to get to my seat in the stadium. It wasn't just about the money spent on tickets, it's that Jethro Tull is my favourite band (alongside Rush, of course).

Isabel thought I was crazy to go to this show, but she didn't want to try and take it away from me, either. There wasn't too much to look forward to in my life at that time.

Anyway, I remembered that, in the stands of this stadium, the armrests did not swing up, and were immovable. There was no way I was going to be able to get to the centre of the row. My plan was for us to arrive early, and see how the Customer Service people could help. One idea I'd had was that Scott and I would steal the seats on the edge of the row, even though it was a downgrade from the centre. When the edge seat owners came along, I would congratulate them for being upgraded to the centre of the row.

But the Customer Service people had a better idea. The manager, a young fellow named Ryan, took a hold of me and my wheelchair and asked Scott to follow us. He took us down to the third row (after verifying our tickets) and we saw that the entire front section had folding chairs—no armrests! There were also no people in my way, as the rest of the row's fans hadn't arrived yet. So, I power-lifted myself from my wheelchair onto Seat Number 1. There were a total of 20 seats to the centre. Ryan sat beside me and hauled me across each seat. He let me use his forearm for strength and balance. After a couple of breaks (for me), we arrived at Seat 21. I was all set—except that my body was finished. I was in a great deal of pain from my trek across the chairs, and I wanted to go home. I watched as other people filled up the chairs on either side of me, and I knew I would remain where I was until the end of the show.

Ryan had taken away my wheelchair, and he returned shortly with a couple of water bottles for Scott and me. He then presented us with $30 in vouchers for the food stands. I gave everything to Scott and Craig. I couldn't eat or drink, as I had to be very careful of my bladder and my bowels. I was essentially trapped in my seat. But before I'd had a chance to effectively feel sorry for myself, the band blasted onto the stage. Sitting this close was exhilarating. At around the halfway point of the show, I had to rest my head on Scott's shoulder, using my sweater as a pillow. I still saw the entire show, but I was too weak to clap between songs.

Eventually, after playing "Locomotive Breath" as an encore, the band fled the stage. I then realized my new predicament. Even after everyone left Row 3, I did not possess the strength to shimmy across 20 chairs, even with Tough Guy Ryan to help me. "Are you ready to go?" Ryan's voice came from over my shoulder. He had removed a bunch of folding chairs from BEHIND me, and he had my wheelchair with him. Then Craig arrived, so we could all leave together. Within seconds, Ryan was pushing me up the ramp towards the exits. Then he made an unexpected left turn and unlocked a gate, bringing us out via a private way, by the transport trucks and a tour bus, bypassing the crowds. Ryan even went so far as to accompany us out to Scott's car before he took his leave with my undying thanks. It was a great night among friends, a great show—and I survived it.

July 23

Since I came home from the hospital in March, Isabel has been looking after me. She took a leave of absence from work. Combined with the fact that I no longer had my music school (the payments for which would not start arriving until later in the year), money was starting to get very tight. Knowing this, my sister, Jenny, offered to start a campaign with the website, Go Fund Me. This allows people who care about me or my situation to donate to my cause. I was not at all comfortable with the idea. A number of kind friends had recently asked me if they could hold a benefit concert for me, but I politely declined. In the end, the website campaign seemed to be the best way to go. Jenny composed a short paragraph outlining my situation, and somebody came up with a photo to post with it. The problem with the photo was that it had been taken back in the days when I was resilient. In that pose, I looked as if I were ready to climb Mount Kilimanjaro. In the end, they decided on a picture of me smiling from my hospital bed. News of the campaign spread through Facebook, and people came out in droves, donating what they were able. In the end, my sweet sister presented me with a sizable amount of money. But what really made the whole thing special was the incredibly kind words that people wrote on the site. I tried to read as many of them as I could. Jenny, in her turn, took the time to reply in thanks to every one of them.

August 3

For last Christmas, I bought my 12-year old daughter, Meghan, two tickets to go see the singer Taylor Swift in Toronto. The show wasn't actually until August, but I was planning to take her. Then came spinal surgery, and my wheelchair. After seeing how difficult it was for me to get to and from the Jethro Tull concert, I knew that I could not take her myself. So I called on my sister, Meghan's Aunt Jenny, to take my daughter, and she readily agreed. Jenny's youngest daughter, Rebecca, is the same age as Meghan, and she also likes Taylor Swift. So Jenny tried to figure out a way for both 12-year olds to go to the concert. A couple of people had suggested Jenny take the two girls to the venue and send them in on their own. But the show was at the Skydome (now called the Rogers Centre), downtown Toronto. There wasn't a chance in Hades that Jenny and I would allow our little girls to wander around the stadium on their own. In a crowd of 18,000 people, who knew how many ne'er-do-wells would be in attendance, looking for girls who appeared vulnerable. In the end, Jenny called the ticket company and traded the two tickets for a set of three tickets at the same price. All was good—except for the fact that I had to miss out being with my daughter at the show. But the girls were in great hands with Jenny.

They took the GO Train into Toronto, so as not to have to worry about parking. The concert was apparently very well played, and the girls (the three of them) sang along to most of the songs. After the encore, Jenny brought the girls back to the commuter train station to catch a lift home. The little ones were exhausted, and trudged along. But Jenny knew there was a train home in two minutes, with the next one leaving an hour after that. So she convinced the girls to high-tail it to the platform, which they did, however grudgingly. In the end, they made it to the train on time, getting home at 1 AM. It took a couple of days for poor Meghan to recuperate, but she's got great memories of the concert.

August 5

I recently had a CAT scan, and I was quite worried about the coming results. When we saw Dr. Hotte, he reported that the chemo caused nearly all the tumours to reduce in size. The lone exception was my liver. It still had many tumours in it, three of which were quite large in size. Dr. Hotte looked into radiation but, alas, he found that it would apparently be ineffective. With heartfelt compassion he said to me, "You need to understand that this cancer will take you. You probably will not see Christmas. You will die of liver failure."

August 16

Since June, I've been out of it, out of my mind, and terribly weak. I scared Isabel, who figured my days were numbered. I had no idea what was going on around me. I just knew that I spent a great deal of time being confused, and it was confusing to those nearby. I had no fear of dying at this point because my thinking wasn't clear enough to comprehend the idea.

My breathing had become laboured, and I used an oxygen tank with a nasal tube to help me breath more easily at night. My legs were swollen because there was so much cancer in my liver. I could hardly talk, and I knew very little about what was going on around me.

I have a VON nurse who comes to my house twice a week to check up on me, inquiring after my health and well-being. The poor girl came once when Isabel had stepped out for a while. She asked me her regular series of questions, and I answered "I don't know" to all of them:

"Have you vomited recently?"

"Uh, I don't know."

"When was your last BM?"

"I have no idea."

Around the middle of August, I was able to start taking a higher dosage of chemo. Dr. Hotte also arranged for me to have a calcium infusion, as my calcium was very low (this often leads to confusion). Soon, I started to come around and become myself again. It was very refreshing, and Isabel was overjoyed to get her husband back.

August 26

It was a Sunday morning at 5:30 AM, and I woke up with a funny tickling on my upper lip. I touched it and came away with blood. It turned out I was experiencing the beginning of The Nosebleed To End All Nosebleeds. I woke up Isabel, as I was unable to stop the dripping. I did the regular things, pinching my nose and holding my head forward. We called Ontario Tele-health to speak with a nurse for some advice. During the discussion, the dripping increased to a steady flow, like a faucet half opened. Before long, my nightshirt was covered with blood, as were both my arms. I looked like I had been shot several times in the chest. Isabel gasped, and the nurse on the phone went ahead and transferred us to 911 Emergency.

The ambulance arrived shortly, and I was taken away to the hospital once again. The poor EMT who stayed with me in the back of the vehicle clamped my nose shut with her gloved fingers, and it hurt like hell. She explained that it was necessary, in order to stop the flow of blood. Right after we drove out of my neighbourhood, the driver put on the flashing lights and sirens, and the ambulance tore through Dundas towards Hamilton. I called out to the driver to turn off the siren, as it was early, and people were trying to sleep. The EMT in the back with me just smiled, and suggested I let them do their job.

Once we reached Emergency, I had to wait for only a few minutes before being admitted. My entire torso and both arms were covered with blood, and people in the waiting room looked at me as if I had been shot or stabbed, as if I were about to die right then and there. In response to one fellow staring at me, I said, "Well, you should see the other guy."

The nurses somehow got my bleeding to stop. The doctor shoved an enormous amount of packing up my nose. It was to remain there for two or three days. Then they cleaned me up and put a hospital gown on me. It then occurred to me that I should have asked someone to take a photo of me with The Great Nosebleed of 2018. But we had been panicking, and it wasn't really on our minds at the time. Had we done so, I'm not sure the photo would have made it to this book, but I would have had some fun with it.

For one of my school's movie-making camps a few years ago, I had a bottle of fake blood for a couple of scenes. The stuff was so realistic, so properly viscous, it was kind of freaky. One of the children in the film asked if he could smother some of the "blood" all over his arm to freak out his mom when she came to pick him up at the end of the day. Then all the kids wanted to do the same thing. So they all made themselves looked wounded. It was so realistic that I had to call every parent and warn them in advance that their kids were playing a joke on them. Even so, some of the moms and dads got a little freaked out when they arrived. Good times.

Back to the present: after things calmed down, it had been determined that I had lost an inordinate amount of blood, so I was taken upstairs to have a blood transfusion—two units. Going home, I was thoroughly exhausted. But at least I had a new story for my book.

August 31

During the past several weeks, everyone thought I was a goner, that I wouldn't make it to the end of the summer. Isabel, my family, the VON nurse all felt it. Me, I had no idea what was afoot. I was just trying to make it through each day. Sometime in August, Isabel had me sign some papers while I was ill. Although she explained what they were for, I didn't take in any of her words. One has to just trust one's spouse. It wasn't until September, when, in a moment of clarity, I happened to check my bank account online and notice that my savings was all gone, that it had all been transferred elsewhere. So I called Isabel over to look at my screen, hoping she may know what had happened. She explained that she had transferred it to her own bank account.

In response to my inquisitive look, she explained, "I didn't think you'd need it, where you were going."

"Oh, okay," I said, and went on with my day. I knew she was doing what was best.

September 1

It felt really good to be out of my long funk. All through the spring and summer, I didn't take calls, I ignored texts and emails, and I stayed away from my computer. This afternoon I logged onto Facebook for the first time in months. I saw that a friend had posted something in the Dundas Music Club's Facebook page. I read the post, clicked "Add Comment", and proceeded to cheekily correct the person's grammar. Within minutes, Danny, one of the club's organizers, replied beneath my comment: "Look everyone: Steve's back!" Indeed I was.

September 2

On Facebook, the majority of my friends are in the entertainment industry. And so people often reach out, looking for singers, dancers, painters—and actors. Today, Kyle, one of my fellow FB film-makers, put out a casting call for the lead male in his next film. A bunch of guys had already replied, so I answered thusly:

> *Go ahead and cancel everyone else, Kyle—I'm your man. Is it okay that I'm in a wheelchair full-time? Also, my Chemo makes my voice squeak, so I often sound like Mickey Mouse. Anyway, see you on set. No need for an audition, screen test or rehearsals. Can't wait!*

September 4

This evening, I held court at the Wellwood House at this month's cancer group meeting. They are a great bunch of guys. I missed a few meetings, as I had been in a bad way, health-wise, between June and last week. Usually if a member doesn't show up a couple times in a row, everyone fears he may have succumbed to his disease. Since I joined up, we've lost two guys.

The last time I'd gone to a meeting, I felt like crap. I stared at my untouched slice of pizza and ignored everybody. It was a stark contrast to my usual talkative self, and it scared the guys more than my extended absence. In any case, they were glad to have me back yesterday.

September 12

I've been playing guitar for 36 years, and so I'm pretty good at it. Last January when I was rushed to the hospital in an ambulance, Isabel brought my health card, toothbrush, etc., but neglected to bring my guitar – I guess there wasn't room in the ambulance for it. Anyway, aside from the occasional visits from fellow musician friends who showed up with guitars in tow, I didn't play while in the hospital, as I didn't possess enough energy. When I was sent home in March, I also didn't play, nor did I touch my guitar throughout the spring and summer during which I was incredibly ill. By mid-August, during one of my appointments with Dr. Hotte, he asked about my guitar playing. I told him I hadn't touched it in months. So he insisted I pick it up again and start playing. "I want you to do a minimum of fifteen minutes a day. Doctor's orders."

Back at my house, I picked up my Fender Stratocaster, and found that I couldn't play. I was very distressed by this. My brain knew what to do, but my fingers wouldn't obey. So I had to basically start over, slowly reimagining the songs I used to know so well, songs I'd played without thinking.

The progress was painfully slow at first, but I eventually arrived at the point where I could get through an entire song, then another and another. I decided I had to show Dr. Hotte the fruits of my labour, the results of his insistence that I play. So for my September appointment, I packed up my electric guitar to bring to the Juravinsky Cancer Centre and, because I never do things the easy way, I had Isabel load my little practice amplifier into the car.

When we pulled up to the front doors of the JCC, I hauled my gear out by the front door, while Isabel went off to park the car. With my vinyl guitar case slung over my shoulder and the amp balancing on my walker, I made my way through the building and waited in line to check in.

Upon being shown to the examination room, I plugged in and tuned up. When Dr. Hotte arrived, I played him the song "Closer to the Heart" by the band Rush. He was very happy to see my progress.

September 20

My son, Blake, is 14, and has just started high school. This evening, he and I sat for an hour on our front porch, talking about girls, booze, and other manly things swirling around in his head. I wouldn't trade that time for a shiny new Cadillac.

September 22

Isabel and I go swimming twice a week at a nearby old folks home, and it's awesome. The plan was for her to just wheel me to the edge of the pool, lift up the back of the wheelchair and plop me into the water. But the place we go to has a hydraulic lift. Sometimes we go during a water fitness class. In the photo, there are several old ladies—and Steve. But I don't do the fitness class; I'm there to frolic. It's amazing for me because I can kick my legs out and exercise them. I can even walk, when I go to the 4-foot depth (buoyancy is my friend). Isabel took a couple of snapshots of me in the water. It's crazy how skinny my arms (and legs and chest) have become. I miss being muscular, filling out my T-shirts. Oh well; at least I can pretend I'm Aquaman.

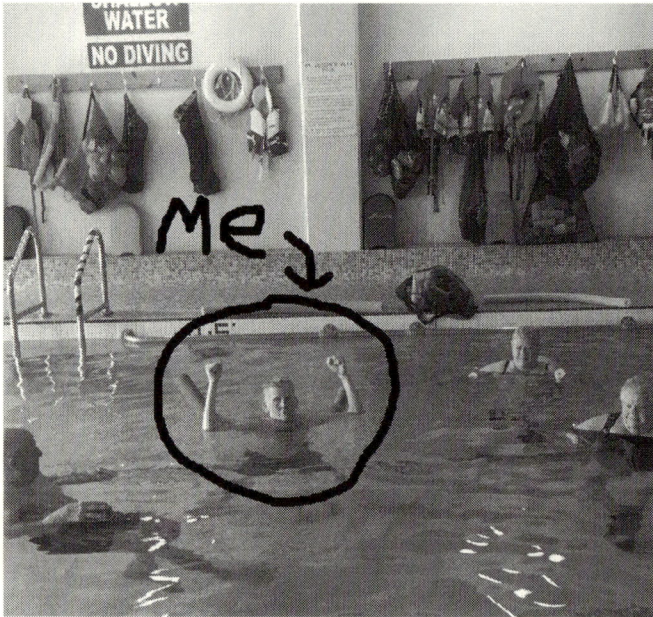

October 8

Humpty Steve wanted it all.

Humpty Steve had a great fall.

Yes, indeed. I was doing my morning exercises using my alpha-walker, by myself, with no one to spot me. This is because I'm invincible. Anyway, I lost my balance and buckled over, falling spectacularly to the ground. I landed on my back and bonked my head on the floor. I called out in pain, and cursed like a sailor. My daughter, Maggie, came right over and admonished me for my potty mouth (after asking if I was okay). With bruises to my body and my ego, Isabel hoisted me up to my wheelchair so I could recuperate. After a while, I continued my exercises, with my son, Blake, spotting me. Now they're singing to me: "Humpty Dad had a great fall."

October 17

Earlier in this book, I talked about the Dundas Music Club. It's a fantastic place for professional and hobbyist musicians alike to converge and play songs. My friends Danny and Jay do a stellar job putting it on. I hadn't attended a session in over a year, what with being in the hospital and then in a wheelchair. But I decided that I'd waited long enough, and I wanted to go again. The problem was that the club is held in the basement of a local building, the Oddfellows Hall, and the stone steps are narrow and difficult to navigate. So I posted on the club's Facebook page, asking if there were any tough guys who could carry me down the stairs (and back up after the show). A few fellows agreed, including Denis Fleming and Stephen Brown from Fleming Martial Arts, and Artie McConnell – all tough guys.

When it was my turn to play, I did my two songs, after which I was ready to pass out from exhaustion. So the boys hauled me and my wheelchair right back up the stairs. Isabel followed behind us, biting her nails for fear of me being dropped. The guys delivered me to my car. In the end, it was just another great night.

October 18

I decided to start planning my funeral. This was not to be a concession of defeat. I thought back to the previous summer, and how I had been too out of sorts to properly access my brain's ability to think coherently. But now that I was feeling better, I decided to do something constructive and put some ideas together for the party that would possibly happen after I died. Besides, Dr. Hotte had made it clear that my days were numbered.

I hid this task from Isabel, as I knew it would only make her sad. But doing these things empowered me. So much of my life is out of my hands; it felt good to be able to maintain a semblance of control. I put together a budget and I wrote my obituary.

My musician friend, Annette Haas, came by for a visit. I'd asked her if she could do a song for my funeral (whenever that may be), and she played a piece on acoustic guitar, something she had written a little while back. It was one of the most beautiful songs I'd ever heard, worthy of a Paul Simon comparison. At the end, I wiped tears away and said to Annette, "That's the song I need." I'm sure there won't be a dry eye in the house when she performs it. I also booked my friends Wayne Krawchuk and Danny Medakovic to sing as well.

October 23

I went shopping at Fortino's grocery store today by myself (kind of). I had a small red shopping basket on my lap as I manoeuvred my way around the colossal store. It was amazing how many people (other patrons) offered to help me grab things out of my reach. At one point I became tired, somewhere in the produce section, and I stopped wheeling my chair, so I could rest. A fellow asked if I was okay, and I told him I just needed a break. He then grabbed the handles of my chair and started pushing me.

"Where to?" he asked.

"Why, the ice cream section, of course." Okay, I didn't actually say that last part, but I got delivered to where I needed to be. It's all about the kindness of strangers, sometimes.

It's interesting, because I understand that some people who are in a wheelchair for life may not appreciate being pushed around by a stranger. In my case, I was happy for the help.

November 1

Buckle up for something heavy. I read in this morning's *Spectator* about the problems with Canada's assisted dying laws. Halifax's brave Audrey Parker will be dying today, against her wishes, but within the parameters of the flawed law. Myself, I know that my demise will be the result of metastatic liver failure due to kidney cancer. I have no desire to have a doctor end my life—I'll go when God takes me. But what if the disease becomes unbearable? One option is for the patient to have food and water withheld. That sounds crazy, a horrible way to go. Fuck cancer. But this is not something I need to deal with today. It's time to turn my attention to the leftover Hallowe'en candy.

November 2

This was the day the movie *Bohemian Rhapsody* (the rock biopic of the band Queen) was to be released). I went to the theatre with my entire family, as we all love Queen—even my kids and their cousins. One element of our outing involved the fact that, at one point, I was not supposed to have been around long enough to see this film. One of the recent predictors of my demise had me leaving this planet before the film's release date. Yes, I was upset about leaving my wife and kids behind, but missing this film because of cancer was starting to piss me off. Luckily, I made it this far. The movie was great. For me, we all had to sit in the front row, as that's where the theatre has space for a wheelchair. After the movie was over, my brother pushed my chair out to the exit. There are about eight or ten steps to get down from the parking lot, but I naturally took the ramp. I told Chris he could let go of me, and I flew down towards the bottom of the ramp, picking up speed as I went. By the time I reached the landing, I couldn't stop, and I careened out to the parking lot. Two cars saw me coming, and screeched to a halt, so as not to run me over. I eventually levelled out and slowed down, with my kids and nieces running after me. It was actually the most fun I'd ever had in a wheelchair. But my poor brother was not impressed.

November 5

I was alone tonight. Not to be overly dramatic, but I hadn't been alone overnight since late 2017. Isabel works many night shifts, so I'm well used to having the house to myself. But there were many times last year (when the tumours had attacked my spine) that I had friends spend the night, when Isabel was at work, and I couldn't be alone.

After my extended hospital stay last January to March, Isabel took a leave of absence from work, and has been looking after me, so I was never alone. But in the past couple of months, I've been gaining independence, rocking my wheelchair around the house like a boss. I knew I'd be fine tonight, but if I had any trouble, I hoped to be able to call Cam or Sally to come over and maybe read to me.

November 10

Today, I am Hercules (though maybe not as muscular). I've been in a wheelchair since my spinal surgery in January, and I've been unable to ascend a single stair. But I've been exercising every day, swimming twice a week, and I have a great physiotherapist. Bit by bit, I've been able to stand for a few moments or walk a couple of steps. My walking is just like that of Tim Conway's old-guy character on the *Carol Burnett Show*: "I'm moving as fast as I can..." My problem is that stairs are my enemy. I've had to miss out on many events because of being stuck in a wheelchair. Today, I'd decided I'd had enough. Plus, I've gained a good deal of strength, of late. With my buddy Cam spotting me, I made it to the upstairs of my house for the first time in a year and a half. Previously, I had to take my kids' word for it when they told me their bedrooms were tidy—not anymore.

Tomorrow, I will receive an award from the Hamilton Film Festival, and I'm going to accept it on my feet. What a great day this is.

I sent the above passage to my doctor friend, Brian. He replied, "F***king Eh! Aren't you supposed to be dead?"

About this photo: after I'd made my way up and then down the stairs, I asked Cam to take a photo of my triumphant accomplishment. I peeled off my shirt (to show all my "muscles") and struggled my way back up to the fourth step, hanging on to the railing for dear life. I turned around and, when Cam had the camera ready, I let go of the railing for a brief moment and crossed my arms in victory. I waited to hear the click of the camera before I grabbed hold of the railing again; it wouldn't be cool to be photographed tumbling down the stairs.

November 14

I am never sitting in that wheelchair again. Hearing me say this, Isabel asked if that was because I'm feeling strong, or because I'm obstinate. I replied that it was a bit from column A, a bit from column B. Don't get me wrong: I'm so grateful to the Cancer Assistance Program who gave me the chair for as long as I needed it, but now it's going go to someone else. I think I'll take Isabel out dancing tonight.

November 19

Today, I had the best MRI experience ever. This was to check out my spine, as I'd had a good deal of extra pain there, lately. At 6:30 in the morning, I checked into the Hamilton General Hospital. Before getting wheeled into the big donut machine, the girl asked me if I wanted headphones with music. Damn straight! Anything is better than that crazy loud beeping sound from the machine. To top it all off, she gave me my choice of genres: 50's, 60's, 70's, country or Classical. I picked 70's, of course. Before retreating to the safety of the back room, the girl gave me a button on a chord, to press in case of an emergency. The music was great: Deep Purple, Gerry Raferty, Warren Zeevon and The Byrds—wait: what? As much as I love The Byrds, they were a SIXTIES band. This seemed like a good time to hit the Emergency button. Luckily, the machine finished its work, and I decided just to leave it be.

November 20

I showed up at the pool at the old folks' home for my twice-weekly swim. Only, this time, Isabel and I went to our separate change rooms, what with me being able to use a walker, and walk a few steps unassisted. After the swim, the old fellows and I hit the change rooms. During my shower, I realized that I couldn't do everything on my own, so I shouted out to the men from behind the shower curtain: "Hey, fellas. My wife's not here to wash some of my bits that I can't reach. So who's going to volunteer to help me?" The chorus of harrumphs was quite funny, as the guys weren't certain if I was kidding or not. Someone ventured a, "Not on your life, kiddo."

December 14

The day was rainy and dark as I headed to the hospital for my CAT scan this morning. It was a scheduled test to check on the state of the tumours.

The nurse was a sweet girl; I'd dealt with her at my other scans. As she did my IV, she remarked about what a miserable day it was outside. I replied with a phrase my father had taught me: "Well, any day above ground is a good day." The nurse stammered a bit, and apologized for being insensitive. I let her off the hook, though. Since having this new lease on life (really, this cancer was supposed to have taken me years ago), I'd decided to not be bothered by little things, like the weather, a spider in the house, too many TV commercials, and so on.

December 15

For the past couple of months, I've been working so hard for my independence, specifically from Isabel. She'd been waiting on me hand and foot. But with each passing day I've been able to do more for myself. I'm pretty close to being a regular useless husband, instead of the deluxe version of a useless husband she brought home from the hospital last March.

December 16

Fernando Lima and Lara Housez live in Dundas, and they are world-class opera singers. They were to perform a show for which guitar accompaniment was required. A few weeks prior, Lara had asked me if I was up to the job of playing with them. Throughout this past year, I'd turned down many gigs, and I was most unhappy doing so. But I was determined not to let this show pass me by. Lara sent me the sheet music, and I got to work. At our rehearsal, the three of us connected well. Fernando was a gentleman, and he and Lara were fantastic.

When the day of the show arrived, I had to think about what to wear. I'd worn pyjama bottoms exclusively for over a year, but I knew I'd have to step it up for this concert. So I pulled out my dress pants and put them on with a bit of difficulty. I stood up, and they slid down to my ankles. Eventually, I went with a pair of black corduroy pants, held up with a belt in which I had to cut a new notch.

The show was great. It was a packed house. By the end, I was in dire pain, but it was worth it.

December 17

There's someone I deal with regularly who breaks the rules to help me. I can't say who she is, or even where she works. I can say that she's very pretty, and exceedingly kind. I often show up at her place of business looking exhausted, like I'd been run over by a truck, so she lets me jump the queue. I can't name her here, as her bosses may be displeased at the favouritism she's shown me. But she knows who she is, and she knows how thankful I am.

December 19

Isabel was working night shift, and she missed my show. Actually, it wasn't a show, but my musical friends, Kevin and Gerry, performed a couple of songs with me at the Dundas Music Club. By the end of our final song, my back was in agony, right around the spot where the tumour is, where I'd had spinal surgery last winter. Gerry brought me home, and I popped a couple of the high-test opioids I'd had from last year. I called Isabel at work, and she suggested I refrain from trying to ascend the stairs to our bedroom. So I set myself up on the couch for the night.

On the nearby living room table, I had my water bottle, and a medicine bottle with a single chemo pill, to be taken at 8 in the morning. And, in anticipation of waking up in the night with more spinal pain, I also kept the bottle of opioid painkillers on the table. I promptly fell asleep, and woke up to my 8:00 alarm, as it was chemo time. In my early morning haze, I grabbed the nearest bottles full of pills, opened the cap and motioned to pour the entire contents into my mouth. Just then, a couple of my brain cells proceeded to rub themselves together, and I remembered that a single pill makes a different sound in the bottle than a whole bunch of pills. Carefully, I returned the bottle of opioids to the table, and took my single chemo pill. I'm sure that my day would have been ruined, had I chugged an entire bottle of Hydromorphone pills.

December 21

Christmas came early for me. This morning, I received my latest CAT scan results, and things have drastically turned around. The main tumour (near my heart) shrank by 90%—it's 7mm, down from 7cm. All the other tumours are rapidly shrinking and disappearing as well. Dr. Hotte said I am showing the best results he's seen on this drug. Cabozantinib is thankfully approved in Canada now.

Last spring was a different story. The doctor had told Isabel I may not make it to the end of the summer, as the chemo didn't seem to be working well. Now, I can look to the future with a greater degree of certainty. It's still too early to plan my victory party, but I know there will be live music and lots of booze. In the meantime, I think I need to take the kids and the missus on a road trip, or else get a job, run for public office.

~ ~

I feel very lucky that I've been able to dwell on the lighter side of my adventures with cancer. And because I'd wanted this book to be not too heavy, I left out a few stories, some of the horrific things that I went through. I've been made to consider the adage that to suffer is to be human. I may accept that, but it doesn't mean I have to like it.

It's weird; I'd never heard of someone having cancer for such a long period, until I'd met my sister's friend Vanessa, who was seven years into her battle. Prior to that, I'd always thought that people either beat the cancer, or they succumbed to it after a few months. Now, I'm five years into this. It looks like I'll be around for a while, yet.

What happens after we die? This question has been laid at my feet. Cancer is a moving target, as my doctor tries to predict and adjust the date of my demise. Nevertheless, sometimes I get frightened about leaving Isabel and the kids way too early; sometimes I get frightened about the afterlife. I do go to church, and I understand that the Bible is contained almost entirely of words that are to be interpreted. Is there a place where my soul will go, where I can greet my ancestors—or do we become nothing but dust? What about reincarnation, ghosts and angels with harps? I have no idea. But what I do know is this: we will all experience the phenomenon of death. This knowledge makes it a little easier to accept whatever happens after we die. In my mind, this leads to yet another opportunity to live a good life each day, work on the bucket list and try to leave the world a bit better than when I arrived.

To say I retired at age 46 sounds romantic, but I was not really ready to let my music school go (even though it is in good hands, and selling it was really the best thing to do). My savings, along with the proceeds of the sale of the school, would carry us along for a little while, at least until this cancer takes me. Then the life insurance will kick in, and I know that my wife and kids will be fine. But there's another scenario, one in which the doctors are wrong about my prognosis, and I beat the cancer. In that case, I'll have to find a new career. Hmm. Maybe I'll be a writer.

Thanks for reading.

- Steve

Made in the USA
Middletown, DE
16 May 2019